Animals that Hunt

ANIMALS
that hunt

Michael Allaby

HAMLYN
London · New York · Sydney · Toronto

Acknowledgements

Photographs

Heather Angel, Farnham 21 top, 22 left, 23 right, 51 top; Ardea – Brian Bevan 73; Ardea – Hans and Judy Beste endpapers; Ardea – André Fatras front jacket, 57 bottom, 84 top; Ardea – Kenneth Fink title page; Ardea – Gary Jones 92 top; Ardea – C. H. McDougal 57 top; Ardea – P. Morris 33 top, 45 bottom, 59 bottom; Ardea – Ron and Valerie Taylor 42, 43; Ardea – Richard Waller 53 top; Ardea – Adrian Warren 33 bottom; Bruce Coleman, Uxbridge 85 right; Bruce Coleman – Peter Arnold 56 top; Bruce Coleman – Ken Balcomb 90 top; Bruce Coleman – Jen and Des Bartlett 45 top, 90 bottom; Bruce Coleman – Sdeuard Bisserot 11 top; Bruce Coleman – J and S Brownlie 90 inset; Bruce Coleman – Jane Burton 20, 23 left, 24, 25 top, 26 bottom, 27, 30 top, 39 top, 51, 61 top, 65 left, 81 left; Bruce Coleman – R. Carr 39 bottom; Bruce Coleman – Neville Coleman 27, 44; Bruce Coleman – Stephen Dalton 36, 60: Bruce Coleman – L. R. Dawson 94 centre; Bruce Coleman – Francisco Erize 54, 76 top, 78 top, 91; Bruce Coleman – Inigo Everson 87 bottom; Bruce Coleman – M. P. L. Fogden 15; Bruce Coleman – Jeff Foott 65 right; Bruce Coleman – C. B. Frith 27 top, 59 top left, 59 top right; Bruce Coleman – Udo Hirsch 79 bottom; Bruce Coleman – Jon Kenfield 48; Bruce Coleman – Stephen J. Krasemann 29 bottom, 30 bottom right; Bruce Coleman – Gordon Langsbury 61 centre; Bruce Coleman – Norman Myers 13 bottom right, 58, 84–85, 92–93; Bruce Coleman – Graham Pizzey 70, 75 top, 79 top; Bruce Coleman – Allan Power 25 bottom, 26 top right, 46; Bruce Coleman – Hans Reinhard 17 top, 49 bottom, 50 top right, 72–73; Bruce Coleman – Leonard Lee Rue 55 centre, 66 right, 89 right; Bruce Coleman – Harold Schultz 50 top left; Bruce Coleman – V. Serventy 75 bottom; Bruce Coleman – Stouffer Productions 74, 82 bottom; Bruce Coleman – Norman Tomalin 50 bottom, 77 top; Bruce Coleman – Peter Ward 32, 41; Bruce Coleman – Rod Williams 17 bottom, 63 bottom; Bruce Coleman – Gunter Ziesler 52, 61 bottom; Mary Evans Picture Library, London 87 top; Robert Harding Associates, London 86 top; Robert Harding Associates – Wally Herbert Collection 86 bottom; Frank W. Lane – Ronald Austing 67 top; Frank W. Lane – A. Christiansen 71 top, 84 bottom; Frank W. Lane – Peter Davey 69 bottom; Frank W. Lane – Treat Davidson 13; Frank W. Lane – F. Hartmann 10; Frank W. Lane – Karl Maslowski 64 bottom; Frank W. Lane – Philcarol 94 bottom right; Frank W. Lane – D. Zingel 63 top; NHPA 45 top; NHPA – Anthony Bannister 26 top left; NHPA – Jeff Goodman 20 bottom; Oxford Scientific Films 18 top, 18 bottom, 19 top, 19 bottom, 21 bottom, 22 right, 35 left, 37 top, 38, 40 47 bottom, 49 top, 80 top; Oxford Scientific Films/Animals Animals – Leonard Lee Rue 77 bottom; Oxford Scientific Films – J. A. L. Cooke 29 top, 30 bottom left, 35 right, 37 bottom; Seaphot 47 top; Survival Anglia Ltd – 70, Survival Anglia Ltd – Jen and Des Bartlett back jacket, 55 top, 66 left, 76 bottom, 94 bottom left; Survival Anglia Ltd – Tony and Liz Bomford 55 bottom; Survival Anglia Ltd – Moira Borland 89 left; Survival Anglia Ltd – Rod and Moira Borland 82–83; Survival Anglia Ltd – Keith Bromley 71 bottom; Survival Anglia Ltd – Cindy Buxton 62; Survival Anglia Ltd – Bob Campbell 7 top, 83, 94 top; Survival Anglia Ltd – Jeff Foot 69 top, 88 left, 92 bottom; Survival Anglia Ltd – Mary Grant 8 top left, 8 top right, 8–9, 12, 93; Survival Anglia Ltd – Lee Lyon 34; Survival Anglia Ltd – Oxford Scientific Films 7 bottom, 41 top; Survival Anglia Ltd – John Pearson 78–9, 81 right; Survival Anglia Ltd – Dieter Plage 6, 11 bottom, 13 top, 13 bottom left, 67 bottom, 68, 72 left, 78 bottom; Survival Anglia Ltd – Dieter and Mary Plage 64 top; Survival Anglia Ltd – Goetz Plage 88 right; Survival Anglia Ltd – Rettig, Halb and Degen 70; Survival Anglia Ltd – Alan Root 53 bottom, 56 bottom, 76 centre, 82 top.

Illustrators

Ray and Corinne Burrows; Dave Eaton; Mike Young.

Published 1979 by
The Hamlyn Publishing Group Limited
London · New York · Sydney · Toronto
Astronaut House, Feltham, Middlesex, England
Text © Copyright Michael Allaby 1979
Illustrations © Copyright The Hamlyn Publishing Group Limited 1979
WORLD OF SURVIVAL
Registered Trademark

ISBN 0 600 30421 3

Printed in Italy

Contents

Hunters of the world

Above:
The Mugger, or Marsh Crocodile (*Crocodylus palustris*) may in times of drought leave its dried out home and walk a long way overland in search of water. It is a broad-nosed crocodile, suggesting that fish form a less important part of its diet than they do of the slender-nosed crocodilians.

The predators are the animals that hunt other animals for their food; they include among their number some of the most beautiful of all animals, and some of the most feared. The tiger has always represented power and the eagle has been the symbol of military might for several great empires. The bear has suggested strength and endurance. Yet we are curiously selective. The wolf appears in our culture more often as the villain rather than the hero. The Nile crocodile has been worshipped in its day and so have some snakes, but has anyone ever honoured a shark or a squid?

Of all predators, Man is the most voracious. We are the only species that kills for

sport or to eliminate rivals. Only Man uses parts of animals to make luxuries, such as handbags, shoes and cosmetics.

Of course, animals with powerful armament can be dangerous and any creature will try to defend itself if it believes it is being threatened. Even so, the risks are often exaggerated. It is unlikely that any human has ever been crushed to death by an octopus and deaths from spider bites are none too common.

If we can forget our fear then we can look at other animals for what they are, and admire the countless ways in which they have adapted to their circumstances. We can appreciate that hunting is as old as life

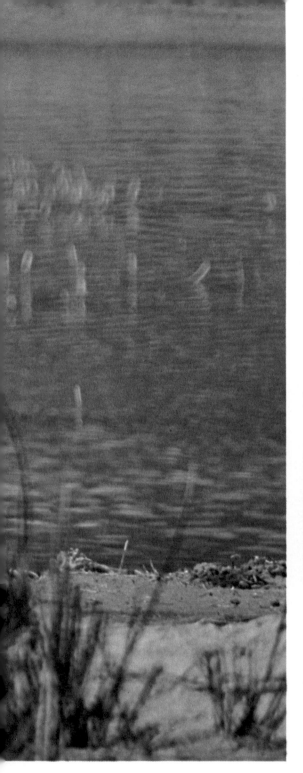

Left:
The lion, like all cats, has a mouth that is well fitted for the life the animal leads. It has a very wide gape, which helps it to seize large prey, and its canine teeth are like sharp, strong daggers. They are for piercing and gripping and the cheek teeth are for cutting. A lion cannot chew its food. Its forward-looking eyes help it judge distances accurately and its sense of smell is keen.

Above:
The ghost crabs (*Ocypode* species) live on the beaches of eastern America. The adults live on land, burrowing into the sand above the high-water mark during the day and emerging at night to feed. They are voracious hunters of small animals, such as the green turtle hatchling seen here.

itself and the relationship between predator and prey, between consumer and producer, is an essential part of the cycle of existence. We may not enjoy the sight of a snake swallowing its victim whole, but we must recognise that its behaviour is no less natural than that of a cow chewing grass, and we may admire the ingenuity with which the snake is able to eat at all, since it lacks limbs or teeth that can chew food.

This book is about the hunters, about the ways in which they live and the forms they have assumed. The story takes us from such primitive animals as jellyfish, worms and snails to squids, crabs, scorpions, spiders and then to the insects. It is among the insects that invertebrate life reaches its highest forms and produces one of its most specialised predators, the praying mantis.

The earliest vertebrates were fishes such as sharks and rays, which continue to compete successfully with more advanced bony fishes. Life moved on to the land, and to the amphibians and reptiles. Birds and mammals are descended from reptiles and, towards the end of the book we follow some of the mammals as they return to the sea, including the Blue Whale, the largest and strongest animal that has ever lived on earth. Finally we must look at ourselves, first as hunters and then as the most dangerous competitors to many of the animals we have met in earlier pages.

Latin names are used in this book because some species have no common names and others have so many that Latin names are either the only names we have or the safest as they exactly define the animal being discussed.

7

A place in the sun

Almost invisible in the gathering dusk, the tiger moves smoothly through the tall grass in search of a meal. Its striped markings, so striking when the animal is seen away from its natural surroundings, form a very effective camouflage. The background colour matches closely that of the vegetation. In different parts of Asia, their only native continent, tigers vary in colour from reddish-brown to almost white. With the alternating dark markings, the effect is to break up the outline of the animal when seen against a background of shadows.

The tiger sees or hears the animal it is to attack and the hunt begins. It stalks slowly, silently and very patiently, taking care not to alarm its victim by a sudden movement or noise. It tries to approach from the downwind side, so that its own scent is carried

away from its prey. At a distance of 20 metres (22 yards) or less it is within range and it rushes its victim from behind. A single blow from its powerful paw will fell a small animal, which will be killed with a bite to the back of the neck. A larger animal will be dragged down and held still by the tiger's claws and killed with a bite to the throat. It is all over very quickly.

The Tiger (*Panthera tigris*) is the largest of all the cats. A male can weigh as much as 227 kilograms (500 pounds) and may measure 4.3 metres (14 feet) in length and stand 1.5 metres (5 feet) high at the shoulder. The female is rather smaller. Tigers are superb hunters, perfectly adapted to stalking and killing animals up to the size of a deer and even, occasionally, a buffalo that is old or weak and separated from its herd. Today, though, you would be very lucky

Above:
The tiger hunts by sight and hearing rather than by scent, stalking patiently from the downwind side of its prey until it is within about 25 metres (27 yards) from which it launches a swift and powerful attack. A small animal, such as the monkey this tiger has caught, is killed with a bite, or a blow from a paw.

Opposite bottom:
The tiger's camouflage. The irregular vertical dark stripes (*left*) against a tawny background disrupt the shape of the tiger, making it difficult to see. If the tiger had horizontal stripes (*right*) it would stand out prominently.

8

indeed to see a tiger in the wild. There are few of them left and all of them may become extinct within the next 50 years, except for those living in zoos.

Despite their power and efficiency, there never were many tigers. They were never numerous like deer, say, or cattle. While the animals on which the tiger feeds can live in large groups and find ample food for themselves, the tiger may walk more than 30 kilometres (18½ miles) in a single night's hunting. Like many hunting animals, the tiger spends much of its time alone, within a territory it marks out and sometimes defends.

Why are there so few tigers? Obviously meat-eating animals cannot outnumber the plant-eaters on which they depend, so the number of hunters in any area is fixed by the amount of food available.

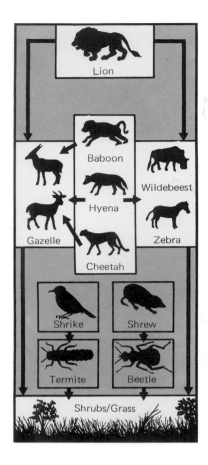

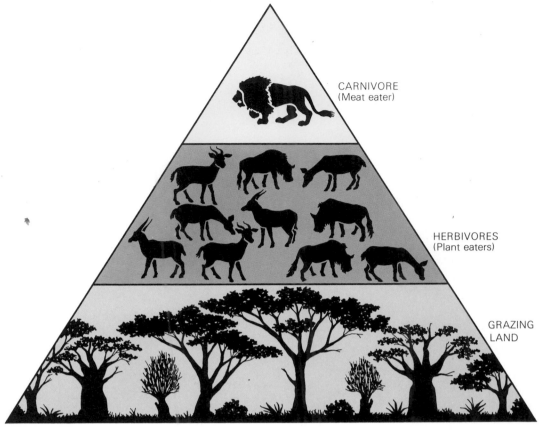

CARNIVORE
(Meat eater)

HERBIVORES
(Plant eaters)

GRAZING
LAND

Below:
Piranhas live in the large rivers of eastern South America, and hunt in groups. They have huge jaws and very sharp, saw-like teeth, those of the upper jaw cutting against those of the lower jaw like scissors, so they can cut pieces of flesh from animals of any size, and are not deterred by thick skin or body armament.

Picture a countryside scene that you know well. It may have fields, perhaps, a pond or small lake and a stream, hedgerows and small woods. Each of these areas of the landscape is different from those next to it. Different plants grow in the field than grow by the stream, and different animals feed on them. Each of these small areas can be examined by itself, as a community of living species, and when it is studied in this way it is called an *ecosystem*.

Our study of an ecosystem can begin with the plants. These are able to use sunlight directly to provide the energy they need to grow. The animals that eat plants, and the carnivores that eat them, all acquire some of this energy from the sun, but at second- or third-hand. Plants use, in most cases, about one hundredth of the sunlight they receive and nine tenths of that is used in respiration and lifting water from the soil. Only about one tenth is used to produce more plant. The herbivores (plant-eating animals) cannot use all of this food, because if they ate all the plants there would be none left to continue growing and to reproduce, and the animals would soon starve. So the herbivores eat about one-third of the food that is available to them. Clearly, there can be very few herbivores compared with the number of plants. Nine-tenths of the energy they derive from their food is used in breathing, in moving their muscles and, if they are warm-blooded, in keeping them warm or cool. Only about one-tenth is used to make cells – tissue that a carnivore (meat-eating animal) can use. Again, if the carnivores were to eat all the herbivores, they would soon starve. They, too, eat only about one-third of the food that is there.

How many plants or animals there are at each level depends upon their individual size. If the plants are trees, there will be fewer than if they were grass. An ecosystem can feed more mice than elephants! So at each level, the total weight of all the organisms is measured. This is called the *biomass*.

If a diagram of this is made, a pattern emerges. First, there is a rectangle whose

width represents the biomass of plants. Above this there is another rectangle, the same depth, but whose width represents the biomass of herbivores, and above that a third to represent the carnivores. Each rectangle is much smaller than the one below it, the topmost one being very small indeed. Within each rectangle the number of individuals depends upon their size. A full grown tiger can eat about 20 kilograms (44 pounds) of meat at one meal, and this is why it hunts in a territory of anything from 65 to 650 square kilometres (25 to 250 square miles). There cannot be many tigers. Piranha fish, on the other hand, are small, the largest growing to only about 60 centimetres (2 feet) in length. For the same biomass there can be many piranhas and in South American rivers they hunt in shoals.

The top predators

These 'top predators' are sometimes called savage and cruel, and people are revolted by the efficiency with which they kill and by the fact that they often kill first the animals that are weak and defenceless. This attitude is mistaken. Carnivorous animals are not fighting their prey because they dislike them. They are not quarrelling, but killing so that they may eat. By killing first those animals that are easiest to kill they make sure it is only the strongest, swiftest and most alert members of the prey species that survive and breed. So that by killing the weak, the prey species as a whole is strengthened.

Where top predator species have declined in number their contribution to the natural balance often becomes very evident. When hunting is reduced, the prey species increase in number. If you look again at the 'food pyramid' you will see that this must overstrain the capacity of the plants to feed them. The herbivores become hungry, then sick. They may try to obtain more food by invading farm lands and destroying crops. Farmers will then be forced to kill them as 'pests', so taking the place of the lost predators. If you kill off the tigers, you may have to become a tiger yourself!

If the predators kill the animals they find most easy to catch, it follows that little by little the prey species will become better at evading capture. This means that the hunters, too, must become more skilled, more powerful, or both. In the case of the larvae of some caddis flies (*Hydropsyche* species) and certain spiders, the hunter has become a trapper, lying hidden to wait for its prey to become enmeshed in the net or basket it has constructed.

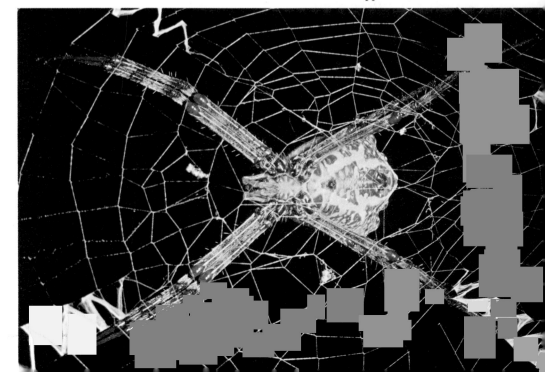

The cats are some of the most efficient of all hunters. They have large brains and are very intelligent. Their fur is coloured to provide camouflage. They can stalk silently and with great patience. Their final attack is very fast. The Cheetah (*Acinonyx jubatus*), the fastest of all land mammals, can run at 112 kilometres (70 miles) per hour for distances of up to half a kilometre. Their teeth are designed to seize and hold, and to cut. They cannot chew. Their claws are designed to hold and tear.

Some birds of prey hunt small land animals in a similar way to the cats. They can lie in wait by hovering in the air, invisible to their prey, stalk by flying on silent wings, their final attack is very swift, and their talons are designed to grip the quarry firmly and their bills to tear off lumps of flesh.

In the water, where concealment may be more difficult, predators have adopted various disguises. The crocodile, lying half submerged, looks very like a dead log as it moves slowly and with barely a ripple to within striking range. The American Garfish (*Lepisosteus* species) drifts through the water lying rigid and looking like a dead stick.

Venomous snakes have a special problem, since they have no limbs and cannot move over the ground as fast as their prey.

Below:
All the cats are capable of great speed over a short distance but they cannot maintain it. The run begins when the hunter has stalked so close to its quarry that further concealment is impossible. This leopard is about to leap upon its prey, it is not running it down as a dog might. Leopards usually hunt and live alone and are mainly nocturnal.

They bite their prey then follow the victim by its scent after it has been bitten, waiting for it to die from the injected poison.

Predators at a glance

Few animals make tools. Most use only their bodies, which are adapted to fit them for the lives they lead. You can learn quite a lot about an animal just by studying its shape and the way it moves.

From a Domestic Cat (*Felis catus*) much can be learned about cats in general.

A full grown cat has six small, sharp incisors in the front of both jaws, at the centre; these are for cutting. On either side of them are the canines, four in all, like

Below:
The Short-nosed Garfish (*Lepisosteus platostomus*) has a body enclosed in thick scales. It drifts through the water hunting for prey and resembles a dead stick.

Above:
The African River Eagle (*Haliaetus vocifer*) lives mainly on fish. Its attack consists of a fast dive that is difficult for the fish to see until too late.

Bottom left:
The Indian Marsh Crocodile, or Mugger, also eats fish, but it will take any animal that enters the water. The carcase in front of this crocodile may well be all that remains of an earlier meal.

Bottom:
The African Boomslang (*Dispholidus typus*) lives in trees and hunts mainly by day. Its name is the Afrikaans word for 'tree snake'. Its diet consists mainly of chameleons. It is the most venomous of the rear-fanged snakes.

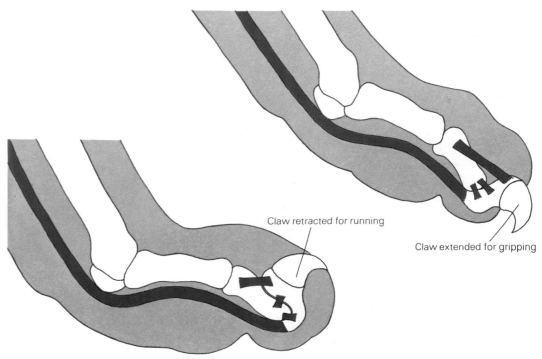

Claw retracted for running

Claw extended for gripping

Right:
All cats except the cheetah can retract their claws. The claw is attached to the last bone in the toe and this bone can swing back over the bone behind it. Its movement is controlled by two tendons. When the top tendon relaxes and the bottom tendon contracts the claw-bone is pulled down (top). When the top tendon contracts and the bottom one relaxes the claw-bone is pulled up to retract the claw (bottom).

Below:
The teeth shown in the skull of this lion clearly indicate its carnivorous diet.

LION'S SKULL SHOWING TEETH

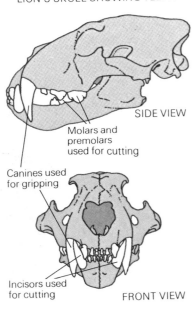

SIDE VIEW

Molars and premolars used for cutting

Canines used for gripping

Incisors used for cutting

FRONT VIEW

daggers or spikes that project beyond the teeth beside them; these are for gripping and they can inflict a deep wound. Behind them are the premolars, three on each side of the upper jaw and two in the lower, and then the molars, one on either side of each jaw. These cheek teeth are sharp-edged, cutting tools. If you look at your own back teeth you will see they are rather smooth and nearly flat on top. They are useful for grinding and chewing. Cats cannot chew. Their teeth cut up food into small pieces that are swallowed whole.

A cat's claws are strong and sharp and they can be retracted. Apart from the cheetah, all cats can retract their claws into a sheath of skin. This prevents them from being blunted when the animal walks. They are attached to the final bone of each toe, which can rotate around the end of the

bone next to it. This end bone is fastened to two tendons, one above and one below, so that by contracting one or other the claw is drawn up and back or down and out.

The cat's face also contains clues. Its eyes open wide and in some species, including *F. catus*, the pupil is vertical. This gives excellent vision in dim light. Both eyes look forward, which provide it with binocular vision as an aid to judging distances. It cannot see to the side but such wide vision is not needed, unlike a rabbit which needs to see every small movement that could warn it of an attack. The cat's ears are upright and alert. Its hearing is keen. Its whiskers are sensitive organs of touch. This combination of large eyes with vertical pupils, large ears and sensitive whiskers, indicate a nocturnal hunter. The cat stalks by night.

Right:
Like all cats, the lion has excellent eyesight. To either side of its head it is aware of small movements which it sees 'out of the corner of its eye' and without moving its head. To the front both eyes work together, producing separate images that are put together by its brain in such a way as to enable the cat to estimate the distance between it and the object it sees. It needs this ability if it is to judge its attack accurately.

Opposite:
The Bobcat (*Lynx rufus*) is found throughout North America from southern Canada to northern Mexico. It may have earned its name from its short tail and lolloping, rabbit-like gait. Rabbits are an important part of its diet; this one has just caught a desert cottontail.

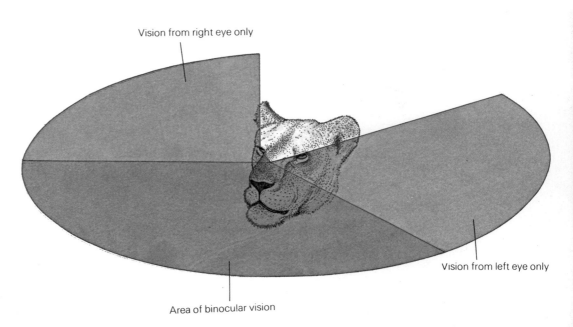

Vision from right eye only

Vision from left eye only

Area of binocular vision

You can translate what you learn from the cat to other species. An owl, for example, has an almost cat-like face, because it, too, has large forward-looking eyes for nocturnal hunting. The eagles and falcons look fierce and aggressive, mainly because their eyes look forward, rather than to the side.

With other birds, it is the bill which shows that they are hunters. For hunting insects, worms and molluscs, birds like the Song Thrush (*Turdus philomelos*) have long, sharp, narrow, and usually straight bills. Birds that catch fish in water, like the Grey Heron (*Ardea cinerea*) have long, powerful bills that look like spears.

A cat may seem nothing like a beetle, but the ground beetles are splendid hunters and they have solved the general problems of hunters in rather similar ways. There are many hundreds of species of ground beetles and they can be found fairly easily, probably hiding by day under a stone or piece of wood. They are all rather large, with very shiny backs, sometimes of a metallic colour. You may need a lens to examine one closely. It will not bite you.

It has long, slender legs, all the same length, for swift running. It locates and identifies its prey by means of large, protruding eyes, long antennae and sensitive mouth parts. When it finds an insect smaller than itself, the victim is seized with its large, powerful mandibles, the claw-like structures in front of its head. Once caught, the insect has little hope of escape.

Right:
Although the owls and the birds of prey are not closely related, their similar ways of life have given them rather similar looks. Both have a curved bill with a sharp upper mandible, for tearing at their food and both have large, highly developed eyes that look forward, giving them binocular vision for judging distances as they attack. Because they hunt by night, the owls have more sensitive hearing than daytime birds.

Top left:
The Song Thrush eats worms, insects and berries, and in spring you may find the 'anvils', usually flat stones, on which it breaks the shells of snails by hammering them. Its claws are strong, for perching, and its feet and legs are adapted for spending much time feeding on the ground. Its bill is strong and sharp, for probing, seizing, holding and pulling.

Below left:
The Grey Heron lives close to lakes and rivers, feeding mainly on fish, although it also catches amphibians and field mice. Its powerful bill is used in a stabbing movement, the bird standing motionless for long periods waiting for unwary prey to come within its range. It cannot make use of cover, for there is none, and it cannot stalk its prey by walking because that would disturb the water. So it stands and waits.

The invertebrate predators

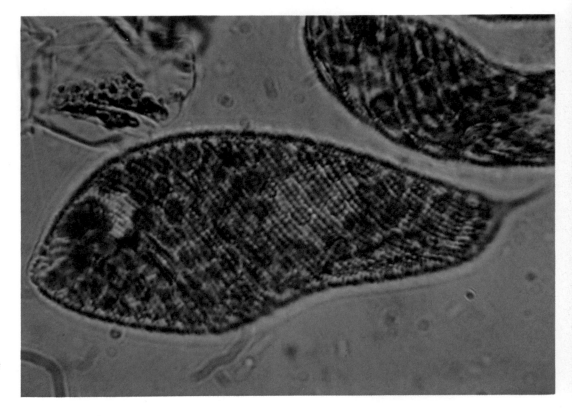

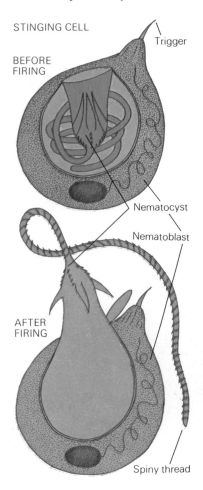

STINGING CELL

Trigger

BEFORE FIRING

Nematocyst

Nematoblast

AFTER FIRING

Spiny thread

The oldest hunters?

Hunting is a way of life that is almost as ancient as life itself. The first, most primitive living things to inhabit our planet consisted of only one cell. They had no hard shells or bones that might form fossils, so what we know of them today is based on the behaviour of their descendants.

If you leave fresh water to stand in sunlight, in time it will turn green. This is due to large numbers of the single-celled Euglena, which contain the green pigment chlorophyll and which will multiply rapidly when conditions are favourable. Some species of Euglena have lost their chlorophyll, and of these some, for example *E. peranema*, have taken to hunting.

Peranema has two simple, parallel rods attached at one end of its single-celled body. When it encounters another Euglena that is not moving, these rods extend and fasten on to the prey, then push it into the *peranema*, which distends itself to 'swallow' it.

Peranema may be the most primitive of hunters and compared with it the members of the genus Hydra are very advanced. Hydra are commonly found in freshwater and the largest of them are just visible to the naked eye. The polyps stand upright, like tiny pins, and when an animal comes within reach they extend many fine threads by which they seize their prey. In some Hydra the victim is paralysed by an injection of poison.

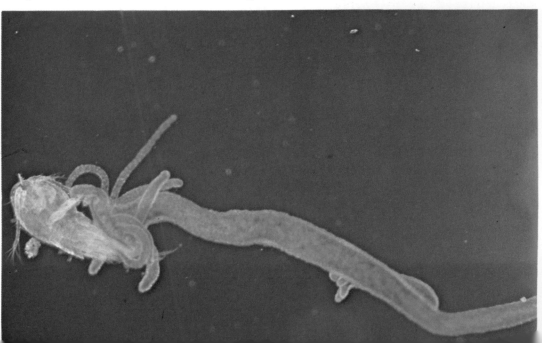

Hunters that sting

Hydra are members of the phylum Coelenterata. All animals in this group are carnivores and have the ability to seize their prey by means of tentacles.

The sting is administered by numerous thread cells called nematocysts which project through the surface of the tentacles. Each holds a sac filled with a corrosive fluid, and when a sensory mechanism is triggered the nematocyst which forms a long hollow thread kept coiled when not in use, is expelled outward, turning itself inside out as it goes.

Most nematocyst threads carry a barb which pierces the skin of their prey and holds it while the corrosive fluid from the sac is injected to numb the prey. Other nematocysts are sticky and this helps to attach the tentacles to the victim.

Hydra, like all coelenterates, do not spend all their lives as hydroids (or polyps) as pictured; they spend part of the time as umbrella-shaped medusae. In some species one or other stage has been almost completely suppressed. Among the true jellyfish, the medusa stage is dominant.

The Portuguese Man-o'-War (*Physalia physalia*) is a colony of hydroids in which each individual has its own function. The nematocysts contain powerful toxins and their sting is dangerous to man. The Portuguese Man-o'-War cannot swim, but drifts with the wind and currents.

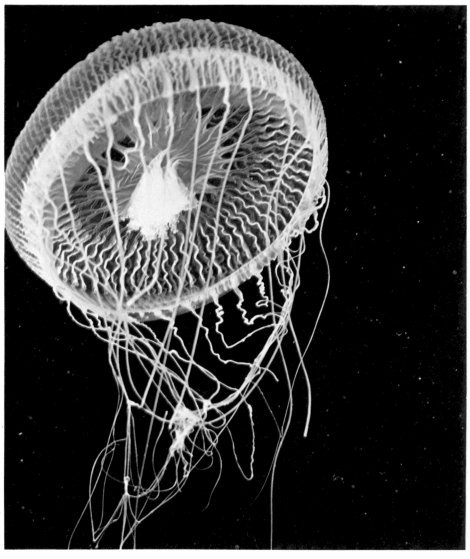

Comb jellies are also mistaken for jelly-fish. In fact they comprise the phylum Ctenophora and evolutionarily they are quite different from jellyfish. They have many forms; most are more or less colourless. The largest grows to about 1.5 metres (5 feet) in a ribbon shape, but most are much smaller. They swim weakly, often in vast numbers, devouring the larvae of many fish and shellfish and other planktonic animals. Comb jellies capture their prey with two tentacles that bear lasso cells, or colloblasts, which secrete a sticky substance. The tentacles sweep the water and carry any small animal they strike to the comb jelly's mouth, where it may be poisoned before being ingested. The Sea Gooseberry (*Pleurobrachia pileus*) is the best known of the comb jellies.

The sea anemones are also coelenterates; they are members of the order Anthozoa. They are more complex than jellyfish, their food is digested in a cavity which is divided into compartments and reached by a gullet from the mouth. In many species digestion begins as soon as the prey is seized and held by the tentacles.

Sea anemones hunt by fanning the water with their tentacles. Each tentacle carries many nematocysts to grip and numb any creature that strikes them. The largest sea anemones can be 90 centimetres (3 feet) across, and their prey includes quite large fish. Once caught, the victim is carried to the mouth of the anemone at the centre of the ring of tentacles.

Because they live alone, sea anemones reproduce asexually, some by tearing themselves in two from top to bottom or side to side, others by detaching a small part from near their base, which grows into a complete animal.

There are many species of sea anemone and although usually thought of as sedentary, that is, staying in one place, many can and do move about. Some drag themselves along like snails. Some turn upside down and walk on their tentacles. Some can inflate themselves and drift. Others anchor themselves to a host, such as a hermit crab, and allow themselves to be carried.

Starfish

The starfishes are much more mobile. Along each of their arms they have tubular feet that can extend in any direction, grip a surface by means of a sucker, and move the animal along.

The starfish has no central nervous system. When one of its arms receives a stimulus that suggests food, that arm begins to move the animal in the direction of the stimulus. Starfish that live in the deep oceans feed on microscopic particles of organic matter, but those found in shallow waters will eat any animal they find, provided the animal is not too large and provided it cannot move fast enough to escape. Starfish eat very large numbers of bivalve molluscs, and will enter fishing nets to eat captive fish.

When they have located their prey, two or more arms envelop it. If it is a shellfish, the two valves will be gripped by suckers on the arms and pulled apart. As soon as they are slightly open the starfish pushes its own stomach out through its mouth, which is at the centre of the underside of its body. Part of the stomach enters the space between the valves and releases digestive juices. These relax the shellfish so that it opens its valves further and the remainder of the stomach of the starfish enters the valves and digests the food. When digestion is complete the stomach returns to the body of the starfish. Small fish are eaten in the same way, although with much greater ease since they have no shell as defence.

The starfishes belong to the phylum Echinodermata, or 'prickly skins', and they have remarkable powers of regeneration, sometimes growing an entirely reformed animal after all the arms have been lost.

Burrowers

Worms have solved the transport problem and many of them are highly mobile. There are many different kinds of worms, and some of them are predators. Bristleworms are members of the same phylum (Annelida) as earthworms. The name 'bristleworm' refers to the bristles on the body, which in

some species can inflict a severe sting. Many bristleworms have eyes, sometimes complex ones.

There are more than 4,000 species of bristleworms. Most of them burrow in the sand and you can see their worm casts at the seaside, below the high tide mark. Some, like the Green Ragworm (*Nereis virens*) which is 20 centimetres (8 inches) or more long, leave their burrows to swim in search of their prey.

The hunter and the hunted

There is nothing about the role of carnivore to prevent the hunter from becoming the hunted. The predatory sea anemones would be much more numerous but for their voracious enemies, the nudibranchs, or sea slugs. Most sea slugs are carnivorous and many are brightly coloured. *Archidoris pseudoargus*, the sea lemon, is typical. It is bright yellow and about 7 centimetres (2½ inches) long. Sea slugs cannot move fast enough to catch a quarry that makes a run for it, but they feed on any sedentary animal they can find, being quite indifferent to poisoned tentacles or to the masses of gritty material inside sponges. When they eat hydroids they cannot digest the nematocysts, however, so they put them to ingenious use, by storing them in a part of their body reserved for this purpose and 'firing' them, like missiles, at any would-be attacker.

The sea slugs are related distantly to the land slugs and to the snails. Many snails

Above:
The ragworms have large jaws with teeth. Some species burrow in sand or mud on the lower shore or in pools, others live at the surface. All are active predators.

Left:
The sea slugs are often brightly coloured and the shell, usually found in molluscs, is either reduced in size or absent entirely. The absence of the shell makes the animal more mobile, helping equip it for its predatory way of life.

Right:
The cone shells are slow-moving
animals, even for snails, but they
compensate for this by having a
radula modified into an array of
poisonous barbs which they use to
subdue their prey. They are among
the most beautiful of shells, but these
animals can deliver an unpleasant,
and in the case of some tropical
species fatal, sting.

Above:
The Common Necklace Shell (*Natica
alderi*) lives on the lower shore and
in the sea up to a depth of about
70 metres (77 yards), where it
burrows in the sand in search of the
bivalves on which it feeds. Here it is
feeding on a Banded Wedge Shell
(*Donax vittatus*).

are hunters, but the most completely carnivorous group is that of the whelks and cone shells. Whelks are spiral-shaped seashells found on sheltered rocky beaches. The largest are found among the tropical species such as *Fasciolaria gigantea* and *Megalotractus aruanus* which can grow to almost 60 centimetres (24 inches).

Like all snails, whelks have a radula, or tongue, that is covered with barbs so it can be used as a cutting tool. In the whelks the radula is used to bore a hole through the shell of another animal; they can then extract the soft flesh through the hole. The Sting Winkle, or Oyster Drill (*Ocenebra erinacea*) is a serious pest of commercial oyster beds.

The cone shells are close relatives, and include some of the most beautiful of all sea shells – and the most deadly. The radula of a cone shell is modified into an array of poisoned barbs which the animal uses to kill its prey.

Molluscs

Slugs and snails, including the whelks and cone shells, are molluscs, members of the class Gastropoda, a name that means 'belly-foot'. The name is not quite fair, because they do not actually digest food with their single foot, but they do look as though they are walking on their bellies. There is another branch of the mollusc phylum, whose members have the head and foot joined together, the muscular foot having developed as arms, or tentacles; they are called the Cephalopoda, or 'head-foot' and the class includes the squids, cuttlefish, nautili and octopuses. All of them are hunters.

At one time, the ancestors of the modern cephalopods had shells, like snails. In the course of evolution this shell became divided into sections and filled with gas, which enabled the animal to maintain an upright position while swimming; it also enabled it to hunt despite the weight of the shell. Only the Pearly Nautilus has retained this shell.

Squids and octopuses

Other cephalopods evolved shells that were reduced, taken inside the body, or dispensed with entirely. The squids have a shell that is reduced to a horny shield beneath the skin and over part of the head, shaped rather like an old-fashioned pen nib. The cuttlefishes have taken their shells inside their bodies, where they are reduced to a gas-filled 'cuttlebone', which can be seen as white 'bones' on beaches. The octopuses have no external shell or bone of any kind.

Like other molluscs, the cephalopods have rasping tongues (radulae), and mandibles that in this class have developed into a horny beak. The beak of an octopus resembles that of a parrot.

Although the gastropod foot has been modified into a set of tentacles, the 'head-foot' is still the organ of locomotion and sometimes it is very efficient. Beneath and behind the head is a cavity which the animal can fill with water by relaxing certain muscles. When this water is expelled with great force through a narrow tube just below the head, the animal is propelled rapidly backwards.

Squids, octopus and all the cephalopods swim backwards and while many of them are fairly inactive swimmers, some squids are extremely fast swimmers. Some can propel themselves so fast that they are able to leave the water completely and glide

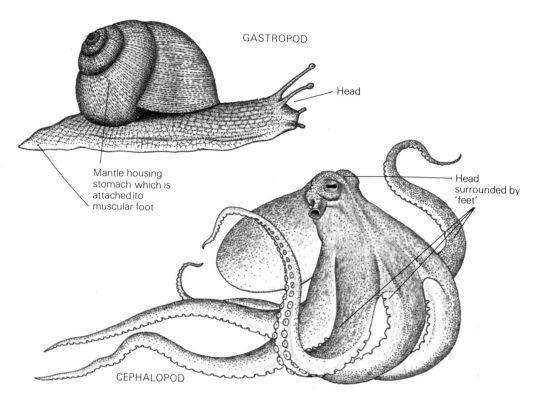

GASTROPOD

Head

Mantle housing
stomach which is
attached to
muscular foot

Head
surrounded by
'feet'

CEPHALOPOD

Below:
Squids have large, highly developed
eyes, which enable them to hunt
efficiently in the dim light of the
ocean depths. The size of the eyes
can be seen clearly in this Pop-eyed
Squid (*Sepioteuthis sepioidea*), a
coastal species seen here swimming
in the Caribbean.

Inset:
The Sting Winkle lives on sand,
rocks or muddy gravel from the
lower shore to deep water.

through the air for up to 45 metres (50 yards) when escaping a pursuer.

All the cephalopods have large, conspicuous eyes. These are truly remarkable in what is, after all, a primitive invertebrate, because they are very similar indeed to the eyes of vertebrates. The eye of a squid is very like a human eye. It may be much larger than the human eye. The giant squid has eyes 40 centimetres (16 inches) in diameter, and in some species the eyes are of different sizes, the left eye being up to four times larger than the right eye. Such highly developed eyes give the cephalopods good vision, which enables them to hunt efficiently in the dim light of the oceans.

The number of tentacles varies. The cuttlefishes and squids are members of the order Decapoda, which means '10 feet'. They have 10 tentacles. Eight of them are short and armed with suckers. The other two are much longer, and flattened and broadened at the end, where each is equipped with suckers and sometimes hooks or claws. The long tentacles can be retracted in many species, but not in all.

The octopuses and Paper Nautilus belong to the order Octopoda, 'eight feet'. They have eight tentacles. In the Paper Nautilus two of them are modified to hold the shell, and these end in large, flat pads. The remaining six, and all of an octopus' tentacles, are more or less of equal length, and all armed with suckers.

The Pearly, or Chambered, Nautili belong to a different order, the Nautiloidea, and they have up to 94 small tentacles, with no suckers.

All the cephalopods can change colour to match their surroundings and while many other animals have this ability, few have it to such a marked degree. The range of possible colours and the speed with which they change are both great. Most animals in this group also have sacs containing an inky fluid that they can eject if alarmed. The ink forms a 'smoke screen' that confuses the attacker and gives the cephalopod a chance to move away quickly and unobtrusively.

Pearly Nautili live in deep waters in a few parts of the South Pacific. They have been caught at depths as great as 900 metres (984 yards). They hunt shrimps and other small animals.

Octopuses feed on crabs and lobsters; these they seize and hold with their tentacles, then break with their beaks or cut with their tongues. There are at least 36 genera of octopus. Some swim freely but many spend most of their time on the bottom, living as crawlers rather than swimmers. They are secretive creatures, tending to hide in lairs from which they emerge when prey approaches. The Common Octopus (*Octopus vulgaris*) which is the most widespread, arranges stones to protect and camouflage itself.

The cuttlefish are nocturnal animals, spending the day buried in the sand and emerging at night to hunt for fish and invertebrates that they find swimming close to the surface.

When the Common Cuttlefish (*Sepia officinalis*) sights its prey it camouflages itself by changing colour. Then it stalks its victim, swimming slowly by undulating its fins and emitting a slow jet of water from its funnel. Its long tentacles are retracted until it is within striking distance, when they are shot out rapidly to seize the prey and carry it to the animal's mouth.

Squids are found all over the world and occasionally they can occur in such large numbers as to constitute a plague. In 1900 such a plague destroyed the crab fisheries

Below:
The Common Octopus spends most of its time on the sea bottom, close to the shore, among rocks and stones. Often it arranges stones to form a lair, emerging when food comes within reach. Here it is about to catch a crab, which it will seize and hold with its tentacles, each of which has two rows of suckers, then cut open with its radula or break open with its beak.

on both sides of the English Channel. Squids hunt their prey by pursuit, although for some species this involves no more than drifting among the plankton. Some squids are luminescent, possibly as a device for recognition and possibly as an aid to hunting. The larger squids use their great speed to pursue fish, darting into a shoal, seizing a fish behind the head with their long tentacles, biting off the head first then eating the remainder of the fish.

Most octopuses are quite small. The Common Octopus is usually about 60 centimetres (24 inches) across, from tentacle tip to tentacle tip. Occasionally one will grow to 100 centimetres (approximately 1 yard). The smallest octopus is the tropical *Octopus arborescens*, about 4 centimetres (1½ inches) across and fairly harmless to anything larger than a shrimp. The largest is probably *Octopus dofleini*, found off Alaska. One specimen had a span of nearly 10 metres (33 feet), but its body measured only about 45 centimetres (18 inches) across.

Most squids, too, are small. The Common Squid (*Loligo forbesi*) grows to about 60 centimetres (24 inches) long, but some squids really are giants. The largest known is *Architeuthis princeps*. One specimen was found to measure about 17 metres (56 feet)

including its tentacles – but it may not be the largest. Octopuses and squids are eaten by many other creatures and the large squids are hunted by the Sperm Whale. Sucker marks found on the bodies of Sperm Whales suggest there may be squids up to 30 metres (98 feet) long. There is no evidence of any larger than this.

Arthropods

The crustaceans, members of the phylum Arthropoda, are almost all aquatic. Woodlice and land crabs are exceptions to this rule.

More typical crustaceans are the prawns, shrimps, crabs and lobsters. Many of these have powerful claws which are used for self-defence as well as for attack. Animals in this group are not usually aggressive, but they must be handled with care because they will attack anyone who disturbs them. Many are secretive and the crabs go to great lengths to camouflage themselves, many carrying seaweeds, sponges or, as in the case of the hermit crabs by living inside an empty shell which is further camouflaged by sea anemones. *Melia tessellata*, a crab that lives in the Indian Ocean, carries two sea anemones, one in each claw, to ward off enemies.

Below:
A Grenadier Crab (*Melia tessellata*) holding Commensal Sea Anemones in its claws as camouflage.

Left:
Cuttlefish sometimes hunt among beds of eel-grass in bays and estuaries. They are difficult to observe because they hunt mainly at night and, like all cephalopods, they change colour rapidly when threatened, becoming almost invisible. This one is coloured to match the vegetation over which it is swimming.

Lobsters and crabs

Lobsters however tend to be scavengers. They are decapods, having 10 legs, eight of which are used for walking, the other two being modified into huge claws.

A lobster will eat anything it can find, alive or dead. It will seize and crush fish, small crabs, molluscs, worms or any other animal that comes its way. The two claws look identical, but they are not. One is a little larger and is used to seize and crush. The other claw is used to scrape the flesh from bones or fragments of shell.

There are more than 4,000 species of crabs. They, too, are decapods in which two of the limbs have been modified into large claws. The main difference between crabs and lobsters lies in the fact that in the crabs the abdomen, which looks like a small tail is folded beneath the body and, in most species, the body is protected by a hard shell called the carapace.

The most familiar crab is the Common Shore Crab (*Carcinus maenas*) famous for running sideways, or 'crab-wise'. Many crabs move in this way, but there are some that run equally well forwards, backwards or sideways, and that appear to use only two of their legs when they are moving fast. Members of the family Portunidae are swimmers, and have flattened feet they use as paddles.

There are a few herbivorous crabs, but like the lobsters most will eat anything they can find, and many species are predators.

They vary greatly in size. Small crabs, *Ebalia cranchi*, for example, measure about 7 millimetres ($\frac{1}{4}$ inch) in length. At the other extreme, the Japanese Giant Crab (*Macrocheira kaempferi*) can be up to 3.7 metres (12 feet) long and the Tasmanian Crab (*Pseudocarcinus gigas*) may weigh 9 kilograms (20 pounds) or more.

Crabs are aquatic animals, but many species have so modified their respiratory system as to enable them to spend much of their time ashore.

The horseshoe, king, or swordtail crabs are not true crabs at all, but are related to the scorpions. There are only five species and the King Crab (*Limulus polyphemus*)

Top:
Like all cracker shrimps, or snapping prawns, this animal stuns its planktonic prey by using its large claw to generate a shock wave in the water.

Top right:
The mantis shrimps live in burrows waiting for small fish to come within the reach of their claws. This one, in the New Hebrides, is carrying sand from its burrow.

Above:
The Squat Lobster (*Galathea strigosa*) is related to the hermit crabs, but instead of living in a vacated shell it lives beneath stones and rocks.

Most of the prawns and shrimps lack claws, but the snapping prawns which do have claws, use them to make a snapping noise that stuns their prey, making it easier to seize.

The mantis shrimps are different. In this group the large pincer-like claws have been replaced by legs, each of which has a final section that has teeth and folds back on itself like a penknife. They live in shallow waters of the warmer seas, where they burrow into the sand or hide in crevices where they lie in wait for any small fish that comes within their range. This hunting behaviour is similar to that of the praying mantis insects, after which they are named.

Left:
Horseshoes crabs come ashore to breed on sandy beaches in spring and summer, usually after sunset and at high spring tides. They feed on worms and thin-shelled molluscs which they pull from the mud.

Below:
A Shore Crab (*Chasmagnathus laevis*) demonstrating its formidable, front claws.

Bottom:
A scorpion's diet mainly consists of insects of all kinds – this small scorpion is eating a grasshopper.

is typical. It lives along the eastern coast of North America from Maine to Yucatán in Mexico. The female grows to a length of about 60 centimetres (24 inches). The male is rather smaller. The King Crab has five pairs of legs. The first pair end in claws, the next three in pincers, and the last pair in flattened spines, used in swimming. At the base of the back legs there is a hard process used for crushing shells, and at the base of the other legs there are processes for biting. All the legs are beneath the body and the animal has four eyes, two above and two below.

All the horseshoe crabs can swim, lying on their backs, but they spend most of their time ploughing through the mud on the sea bottom looking for worms and molluscs.

The horseshoe crabs are often called 'living fossils' because they resemble closely animals that lived in the seas in the Cambrian and Ordovician periods, and because they themselves have not changed in form since the Silurian period, which ended about 435 million years ago.

Scorpions

Among the arthropods, the oldest by far are the scorpions. Fossil scorpions, very similar to those living today, have been dated at up to 350 million years old.

The scorpions are members of the class Arachnida, which includes spiders, ticks and mites. People sometimes mistakenly think of these animals as insects. Arachnids have a body divided into two segments, not three as in insects, and most have six pairs of appendages. Four of these are walking legs, one pair are adapted for grasping prey, and one pair are organs of touch. They have simple eyes, although some are blind. Scorpions may have up to five pairs of eyes. Most arachnids, and all scorpions, are predators.

There are about 600 species of scorpion. Most live in the tropics, but some are to be found living in North America and Europe as far north as southern Germany.

They vary considerably in size. The smallest is about 14 millimetres ($\frac{1}{2}$ inch) long, the largest about 18 centimetres (7

27

inches). They are all formed in much the same way, having a pair of large clawlike chelicerae, resembling the claws of a lobster, four pairs of legs, and a long tail ending in a slightly curved, venomous sting.

Although they prefer warm climates and become sluggish when they are cold, scorpions can survive freezing. They are most common in dry climates, hiding in the ground during dry periods and emerging when rain falls. All of them are nocturnal. They spend the day hidden under stones, or bark, in thatched roofs or in dark, deserted buildings. Except when mating, they live alone and if two adults meet they may fight, often to the death, the winner eating the loser.

Their food consists of insects of all kinds – spiders, harvestmen (daddy longlegs) and grasshoppers, and the larger scorpions will eat animals as large as a mouse. A scorpion can run fast but it does not hunt by chasing its prey. It lies in wait for its approach, then seizes it with its claws, which are also used to tear the food to pieces. It uses its sting only if the prey struggles. The tail is curved over the back and the victim stung from above. This is the only way a scorpion can sting. It cannot sting anything to its rear.

There are countless legends about the venom of scorpions. Some have a sting that is quite harmless to humans. Others, including the large and dangerous-looking *Hadrurus hirsutus* will produce a sharp pain and a local swelling that disappears in about an hour. There are other species, however, such as *Centuroides sculpturatus* and *Centuroides gertschi* of North America and the North African *Androctonus australis*, that are very dangerous indeed, producing a poison that can kill a human in a matter of hours and, in some cases, in less than one hour, unless the sting is treated. The European species deliver an unpleasant sting that is not dangerous unless the victim is especially allergic to the poison. Humans are rarely stung, however, since scorpions prefer to remain hidden, out of harm's way. They are not aggressive towards animals they do not plan to eat.

Scorpions do not need to eat frequently. After a good meal a scorpion can remain without food or water for several months.

Some species are immune to their own poison. Others can be killed by it, but only in very large doses.

Despite their poison, scorpions have many enemies. Reptiles eat them, African baboons have been seen to catch them, tear off the tails, and eat the rest of the animal, and South American army ants will overpower and eat them. Scorpions are their own enemies, too, being cannibalistic.

Pseudoscorpions (order Pseudoscorpiones) are tiny hunters of mites and insects smaller than themselves. There are about 1,500 species and they are found all over the world in homes and gardens. They live on the ground among rubbish, although some species live in caves and one, *Neobisium maritimum*, lives on the beaches of England and France. It is only about 2 millimetres (0.08 inches) long, so it is not easy to find. *Chelifer cancroides*, which lives in houses, is less than one millimetre long. Some species live in old books, and are called 'book scorpions'.

The resemblance between true scorpions and pseudoscorpions is not close. The pseudoscorpions have no tails or stings, but they do have powerful pincers that carry a poison gland opening on to an immobile 'finger' that they use to sting their victims. All are venomous.

The North African camel spider (*Galeodes arabs*), which grows to about 7.5 centimetres (3 inches), is much more formidable. It is not a spider, but a member of the order Solifugae, the wind scorpions; there are about 600 species.

They live in the tropics and sub-tropics, usually in dry places. Unlike the scorpions, they chase their prey, mainly insects of all kinds. They have no poison gland.

The 'Vinegaroon' is also fairly large, reaching about 8 centimetres (3 inches) in length. It looks dangerous because of its long, whip-like tail, but it does not bear a sting. The name was given to it in Mexico because when alarmed it squirts a liquid smelling of vinegar. More correctly named the Whip Scorpion (*Mastigoproctus giganteus*) it lives in the warmer parts of North America.

There are about 100 species of whip scorpions, most of them found in Asia. None of them is poisonous; the tail is a sense organ only. They live in hot climates where they spend the day hidden in crevices or other dark places, emerging at night to hunt. They have powerful pincers with which they grasp their prey consisting of insects and beetles.

There are also tailless whip scorpions (order Phrynichida) and false whip scorpions (order Palpigrada), also called palpigrades. The tailless whip scorpions range from 8 to 45 millimetres ($\frac{1}{4}$ to $1\frac{3}{4}$ inches) in length. The palpigrades are tiny hunters that live in the soil, the largest being no more than 2.8 millimetres (0.1 inch) long.

Centipedes

Although they are neither arachnids nor insects, the centipedes are fiercely predaceous arthropods. Centipedes have been found fossilised in amber more than 50 million years old.

They have long, segmented bodies, with one pair of legs on all but the final three segments. The number of legs varies widely,

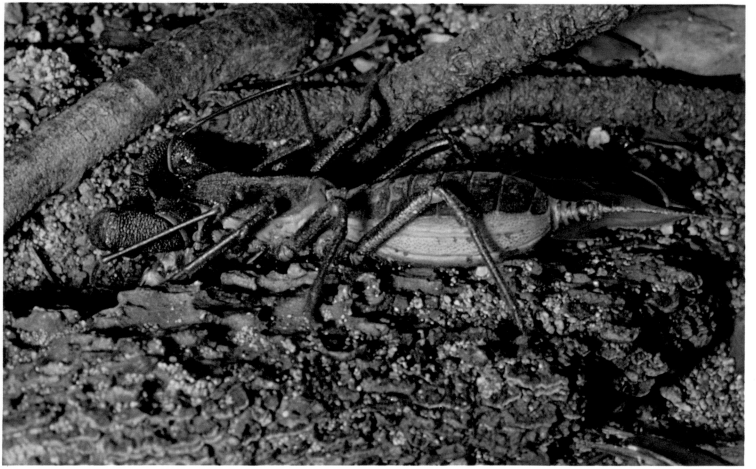

but seldom adds up to exactly 100. The Common House Centipede, *Lithobius forficatus*, for example, has 14 pairs of walking legs and an additional pair at the rear which are used as sense organs. Others, such as *Geophilus carcophagus*, have more legs, the largest number known being 177 pairs.

All centipedes are poisonous, but it is only the very large ones that can harm humans. The bite of some large, tropical species has been known to prove fatal.

Centipedes are nocturnal animals. They shelter in dark places by day, and at night they hunt their prey by chasing it, and the fastest of them can run very quickly. A very few species are herbivores, but most live on insects, insect larvae, slugs and worms, and they are cannibalistic.

Poisonous spiders

All spiders are predatory carnivores and most are venomous, although very few are harmful to Man. The most dangerous spiders are those of the genus *Latrodectus*. They are found in many parts of the world, but the most notorious is the American Black Widow (*L. mactans*), a shiny black spider, often with red markings on the underside in the form of an hour-glass

shape or spots. The full grown female is about 13 millimetres ($\frac{1}{2}$ inch) long, the male 4 millimetres (0.15 inch) or less. The venom of the Black Widow is said to be many times more potent than that of a rattlesnake, but such a small amount is injected that it is very rarely fatal. Young children and old people are affected more seriously than other groups. The bite of a Black Widow produces local intense pain, which may last for some time, dizziness, nausea, vomiting, tremors and symptoms of shock, and breathing may become difficult. The American Brown Recluse Spider (*Loxsceles reclusus*) also has a dangerous, though not fatal, bite. There are other spiders that sting, but the effects do not last and produce no serious harm.

Spider venom is not a weapon of defence and it is not used aggressively. It is a tool that enables the animal to feed on creatures larger and stronger than itself. An insect caught in a web is trapped, but it may be impossible for the spider to eat it if it struggles violently. Venom is injected to subdue it and also to begin the process of digestion.

Tarantulas

The much-feared tarantulas, on the other hand, are quite harmless, although some of them can give a painful bite in self-defence. The original Tarantula (*Lycosa tarantula*) is about 25 millimetres (1 inch) long and lives in southern Italy, near the town of Taranto, from which it derives its name. It was believed that persons bitten by the spider suffered a disease called tarantism, in which they wept, skipped and danced (the dance was called the 'tarantella') and unless saved by the playing of certain music and by magic, they would die. Whatever caused tarantism, it was not the innocuous tarantula spider. In other parts of the world the name 'tarantula' is used to describe large, hairy hunting spiders of the New World, some of which grow to a span of up to 25 centimetres (10 inches). Despite their fearsome appearance, none of them is poisonous and in some parts of America people keep them as pets – even though they can bite!

Spiders as hunters and trappers

There are at least 40,000 species of spiders, living everywhere from the poles to the tropics, and spider populations can be very high. In an undisturbed meadow in England, for example, spiders were found to number about 5.6 million per hectare.

Spiders are members of the order Araneae, in the class Arachnida, and they fall into two broad suborders, the Mygalomorphae, or tarantula-type spiders, and the Araneomorphae, or true spiders.

All spiders spin silk, but not all of them use it to catch prey, and of those that do make traps, the familiar and beautiful orb web is only one design of many. Most spiders live alone; they are voracious hunters. The female is always larger than the male, and mating is a hazardous procedure for the male. To approach the female, the male must make signals that cancel her immediate response to the presence of a creature smaller than herself, which is to eat it. This allows mating to occur, but the effect of the placatory signals is temporary and the hunting instinct soon asserts itself again, so that the male must beat a hasty retreat. Sometimes he does not do so, in which case he is devoured.

Opposite top:
The Malayan Giant Centipede (*Scolopendra morsitans*) is common in the rainforests of Asia, and grows up to 20 centimetres (8 inches) long. It is a formidable hunter of small animals, which it catches by running after them. The first pair of limbs behind the head have poison claws at their tips, from which venom is injected into the victim, which is held securely.

Opposite, below far left:
This female Black Widow Spider is just completing her egg cocoons. First she made a silken sheet in which she laid her eggs. She covered them with a second sheet, clipped the edges together, then made an outer sheet of much tougher silk. In spring, the spiderlings will break out of their cocoons ready for life on their own.

Opposite, below left:
The 'tarantula' of South Arizona spends most of its life in its burrow, emerging to capture large insects and, occasionally, frogs, toads or mice.

Below:
The orb web of the spider is made by:
1. Positioning the boundary lines,
2. running 'spokes' to the centre, then a dry spiral is laid to strengthen the web (3) and finally the sticky thread is laid down (4).

It is this aspect of spider behaviour that earned the Black Widow her name. Spiders that you see are quite often widows!

The wolf spiders of the suborder Mygalomorphae are hunters rather than trappers. They search for their prey and chase it if necessary. They are fast runners and usually larger than the web-weaving spiders. The female carries her young on her back, like a female scorpion, and the young spend their time there until they are large enough to hunt for themselves.

Wolf spiders live in open, well-drained soil, where they dig burrows, sometimes to considerable depths, in which they may spend most of the winter, having sealed the entrance with silk. Their food consists of any animal they can catch and the tropical American spiders of the family Theraphosidae will kill and eat frogs, toads, mice and small birds. There are a few South American bird-eating spiders that build very large, very strong webs in which they catch large insects and small birds, but most bird-eating spiders are typical wolf spiders and chase their prey.

There is also a genus of wolf spider, *Pirata*, which hunts insects on the surface of water. The European *Pirata piratica* makes a silken tube by the edge of the water and hides in it with its forelegs stretched out on to the surface of the water. When an insect alights, the spider detects its presence by the disturbance to the surface, and rushes upon it.

Hunting spiders, such as *Castianeira longipalpus*, are smaller than the wolf spiders, but they, too, chase their prey, which consists of small animals such as springtails.

The crab spiders (family Thomisidae) look like crabs, but they are not related to them. The resemblance is due to the fact that their legs extend to the sides of their bodies, rather than backwards and forwards as in most spiders, and so they run sideways and backwards. They are coloured to match the flower petals or leaves in which they hide while waiting for their insect prey, upon which they rush as soon as it comes within range. Some crab spiders, such as *Misumenoides aleatorius*, change colour from yellow in summer to white in winter and *Misumeria varia* can change between yellow and white according to the flower it is on, the change taking about 48 hours.

The southern Asian crab spiders of the genus *Phrynarachne* are black and white and catch their prey by making a web that looks exactly like a bird dropping. The web is made on a leaf and the spider waits at its centre, usually for butterflies.

Jumping spiders

The jumping spiders, which are marked

with black and white stripes, so that they are sometimes called 'zebra spiders' (family Salticidae) are true spiders, and they use their silk in hunting. Jumping spiders are usually about 8 millimetres (0.32 inch) across, but longer than they are broad. They can run in any direction. They live above ground level, on low plants, walls or hedges, and are widely distributed. They hunt for insects in rather a similar manner to the large vertebrate carnivores, such as crocodiles or cats. When an insect alights in view of the spider it stalks it, making use of any cover available to move very quickly, but otherwise moving across open spaces with great caution so as not to disturb its prey. As it moves it spins and leaves behind it a single thread of silk. When it is within range it jumps down on to the insect, often covering a large distance, considering the size of the spider. Occasionally it misses, in which case its fall is arrested by the drag line it trails behind it and up which it climbs to safety.

Spiders are fully adapted to life on land, and can breathe only air. This has not prevented a few of them from entering the water, however. The Fisher Spider (*Dolomedes triton*) of North America climbs down submerged plant stems to wait for small fish, such as minnows and sticklebacks, which it carries into the air to eat. Like other spiders, the Fisher Spider breathes

through openings in its skin. It is covered with small hairs which trap air that it carries into the water with it. This air supply is sufficient to last for up to 45 minutes.

Since all spiders have spinnerets and produce silk, it is believed that the use of this silk for making traps represents an evolutionary advance. The jumping spiders, for example, leave single strands behind them and if a spider continues to hunt in the same small area for any length of time these strands will become crossed and tangled, forming a primitive kind of web. It is called a 'sheet web' and owing to the haphazard way it is made it has no regular shape or design.

The next stage in the evolutionary process led to spiders that used their silk to make tubes. It is the trapdoor spiders, however, that have developed the technique to its highest perfection. They burrow into the ground, making a tunnel that they line with silk. Sometimes they connect it by strands to nearby plants so that the approach of a potential victim will cause a vibration they will detect. The entrance is sealed with a lid – a trapdoor made from earth, hinged with silk, and shaped so that it fits the opening exactly. The spider waits on the underside, where there are two holes by means of which it can close the door. When it senses, by vibration, the approach of its prey it leaps out very quickly and seizes its victim.

Spider burrows and tunnels are not only traps. They are also used for the animal to shelter from bad weather or from its own enemies, and many species build a tent, either from silk or from a leaf rolled up and held together with silk, for this purpose.

One species, *Argyroneta aquatica*, builds its tent under water. This spider is not large, the female occasionally measuring as much as 25 millimetres (1 inch), including the long legs, the male being smaller. It builds its tent in the shape of an upturned thimble and fills it with air by swimming to the surface, collecting a covering of air around the hairs on its body, then swimming down and releasing the air into its tent, repeating the process until the tent is filled with air. The tent provides it with protection against larger predators, and with a lair from which it can leap upon aquatic insects.

Orb webs

The use of silk reaches its highest level of development in the spiders that weave orb webs. The design of these varies from species to species, but most consist of three or four outer foundation lines that hang from a bridge thread, a number of inner foundation lines, many radial lines, and a hub. The web also has a viscid spiral, a single thread carrying globules of sticky

silk. This is the last part of the web to be made and it is laid in a long spiral from the outside to the centre. The spider waits in a retreat, out of sight, connected to its web by a single strand through which it can sense the vibration caused by any impact on the web. On receiving such a signal the spider will approach, moving fairly cautiously until it is certain the web contains an edible insect.

Spiders use their silk to protect their eggs, and young spiders often use lengths of silk as a means of transport. The young spider climbs to a high place, raises its abdomen in the air, allows a thread to billow out on the wind and when the pull is strong enough, it lets go and floats off through the air. Ballooning in this way, spiders have been known to land on ships more than 300 kilometres (about 190 miles) from the nearest land.

A spider can eat a great deal of food at one time, which it stores in openings off its intestine. It can live on this store for months, or sometimes even for a year or more, without eating again.

Spiders that weave orb webs do not need to see well and their vision is not as good as that of the hunting spiders. Some spiders are blind, but most have three, or more commonly four pairs of eyes arranged in two rows one above the other. Below the eyes are the chelicerae, or pincers, concealing the fang that delivers the poison. The mygalomorph (tarantula-type) spiders move their chelicerae vertically, the true, or araneomorph, spiders move theirs horizontally.

In the temperate regions most spiders live for one year. Males generally live for a shorter time than females. The wolf spiders live longer, however, often for several years, and the large South American bird-eating spiders take eight or nine years to reach maturity. In captivity these spiders have been known to live as long as 20 years. This is very unusual, though. Most die soon after maturing. Like other arachnids, spiders must moult their hard outer covering and all growth occurs during the moult, between losing one skeleton and the hardening of the new one.

Above:
The Funnel-web Spider makes tubes of silk sheeting, often in low-growing plants. These are nests, used to protect the eggs and young of the spider.

Above:
Dragonflies hunt only in flight and
are one of the very few insects that
can hover.

Insects – the most successful animals

What is an insect? The question sounds
silly, because when you meet an insect you
know that it is an insect. Or do you? It is
obvious that a dragonfly is an insect, but if
you were to see its aquatic larva, the
nymph, for the first time would you recognise it as an insect? Why is a beetle an
insect, while a woodlouse is a crustacean?
There are a few simple rules you can use to
place invertebrate animals in their proper
category. If an invertebrate flies, it is an
insect. If it has three pairs of legs, and
antennae, it is an insect. Usually it will have
wings, too, but these may be concealed and
not used. If it has four pairs of legs and no
antennae, it is an arachnid, a spider, mite,
or one of their relatives. If it has one pair of
antennae, many pairs of legs, a distinct
head, and lives on land, it is a myriapod, a
centipede or millipede. If it has two pairs of
antennae and the head is almost merged
with the thorax so it is difficult to see where
one ends and the other begins, almost certainly the animal will live in water, unless
it is a woodlouse, for it is a crustacean.

The insects are by far the most successful
of all animals. Of all the animals alive today,
four out of five are insects. There may be

two million species or more, fewer than
half of which have been described by
scientists. They can be found in every part
of the world. The most common groups are
the beetles (order Coleoptera), the butterflies and moths (Lepidoptera), the ants,
bees and wasps (Hymenoptera) and the
flies (Diptera), but there are many other
orders. Most insects are small, often no
more than about 6 millimetres (0.24 inch)
long, and there are feather-winged beetles
(family Ptiliidae) that measure only a
quarter of a millimetre! The largest insect
that has ever lived is believed to be a
dragonfly with a wingspan of more than 75
centimetres ($29\frac{1}{2}$ inches) which flew among
the trees that grew in forests about 225
million years ago.

Like its modern descendants, those
dragonflies were hunters, living on insect
prey. Many insects live by hunting, and
some are considered to be the most voracious of all hunters.

Beetles

You will find ground beetles under old
wood or stones in almost any garden. Most
are large and black, although some species
are coloured. They are easily identified by
their large mandibles. The minotaur, a still

Left:
Most of the tiger beetles live in the tropics but this one, the Common or Green Tiger Beetle (*Cicindela campestris*) is common on dry heaths and in sandy places in temperate climates. It is a voracious hunter, whose huge mandibles overlap when not in use.

Below:
The ground beetles hunt by night, spending the day sheltering beneath stones, logs, moss or bark. Many, like this one, cannot fly. They feed on earthworms and other insects.

larger beetle, which is not a hunter, does not need these weapons which are used by the ground beetle to seize, bite and tear its prey. The Common Ground Beetle (*Carabus violaceus*) is a member of the largest beetle family, the Carabidae. It feeds on other insects and small worms. There are about 25,000 species.

The tiger beetles (family Cicindelidae) are among the fiercest of hunters. Most are tropical but some, like *Cicindela campestris*, live in temperate climates. The larva lives in a burrow with just the tip of its head at the surface and emerges when a potential victim comes within range, to seize it with its powerful mandibles. The adult, too, hunts voraciously, and flies strongly, fast, but usually for only short distances. It has long legs, protruding eyes and, like its larva, large mandibles. It is smaller than most ground beetles, and coloured green and brown. It lives on sandy heaths and moors.

The diving beetles, and there are more than 2,000 species of them, are found in freshwater ponds. The Great Water Beetle (*Dytiscus marginalis*), common in temperate latitudes, is typical. The adult is an insect about 30 millimetres (1.18 inches) long, and a strong swimmer. It breathes at the surface

Above:
The water scorpions have long 'tails'
by which they hang from the surface
of the water; these are breathing
tubes through which air reaches the
insect. They do not hunt actively,
but hang, head down, waiting for a
victim to come within reach of
their powerful front legs. They feed
on insects, small fish and tadpoles.

Opposite, top:
The familiar Seven-spot Ladybirds
(*Coccinella 7-punctata*) are brightly
coloured as a warning to other
creatures that they are not good to
eat. The ladybirds themselves feed
mainly on aphids.

Opposite, bottom:
The robber fly lies in wait on the
ground or on a leaf until a prey
insect comes within range. It then
makes a short, fast attack, seizes its
victim with its legs, which have
bristles to help hold other insects,
and kills it instantly with an
injection of venom from its
proboscis. It digests its food outside
its body, and sucks the captured
insect dry. This American Robber
Fly is feeding on a bumble bee.

and while it is there it raises its wing covers
a little to capture a store of air that it carries
with it on its next foray. It hunts for insects
and small fish. Its larva, however, is fiercer
still. It hangs by its tail from the surface of
the water, powerful jaws downward, and
it is larger than the adult, reaching about
50 millimetres (2 inches) in length. It can
move about and swim, and it will catch any
insect, tadpole or fish that comes within its
reach. Like many insects, but not its own
adult form, it digests its food externally, by
injecting the prey with its own digestive
juices and then sucking out the liquid,
digested food.

The Water Boatmen (*Notonecta* species),
which grow up to 16 millimetres (0.63 inch)
long, are so voracious that they cannot be
kept in an aquarium with any other animal
unless it is intended that the Water Boatmen
should eat it. They swim on their backs,
rowing themselves with back legs that are
modified into oars, and they dive and swim
under water with great ease.

The largest water bug in the world,
however, is the Giant Fishkiller (*Lethocerus
indicus*) found from India to Australia,
which is up to 10 centimetres (4 inches)
long. Both adults and larvae are aquatic and
feed on insects, larvae, snails and fish.

Popular predators

The ladybirds (family Coccinellidae) are
familiar predators, easy to recognise, and
popular with gardeners because their diet
consists almost exclusively of aphids. So
adapted are they to this diet that they are
slow and lazy in their movements and lack
powerful mandibles, which they do not
need to eat soft-bodied insects. The eggs
are laid close to an aphid colony so that the
ladybird larvae hatch in the middle of an
instant food supply, and they never trouble
to seek other kinds of food.

The glow-worm, which is the female of
the firefly, is wingless and looks like a larva.
There are about 2,000 species in the family
Lampyridae, and the adults eat very little of
anything. The larvae, however, feed on
slugs and snails, which they seize with
sharp, sickle-like mandibles and digest
partly outside their bodies by injecting
digestive juices.

The delicate little lacewings (order Neur-
optera) do not look very formidable, but
next to ladybirds they are the most serious
enemies of aphids. It is likely that the adults
eat little else. The larvae are more adven-
turous and will eat any soft-bodied insects,
and they have been seen to eat mites, small
spiders, and the eggs of other insects.

The hover flies (family Syrphidae) are much stronger fliers than the lacewings. Many of them look like bees or wasps, which they mimic to the extent of making buzzing noises and even stinging motions. No hover fly can either sting or bite, however. They feed on nectar, but the larvae of many species are carnivorous, feeding mainly on aphids.

The robber flies, too, resemble bees and wasps. The largest of them grow to a length of 7.5 centimetres (3 inches). The largest European species is *Asilus crabroniformis*, about one-third this size. All the robber flies are formidable hunters, catching their prey on the wing, and *A. crabroniformis* has been seen to catch, kill and eat solitary bees, honey bees – including queens – grasshoppers and beetles.

Dragonfly larvae, or 'nymphs' take from two to five years to mature and during this time they are fierce aquatic hunters. This nymph is about to seize a water louse by flicking forward its lower lip.

Winged hunter

The dragonflies, though, are the most spectacular of the airborne hunting insects. They are also the most highly adapted to life on the wing. All their hunting is done in flight and some of them can hover. They like the sunshine, some species seeking shelter the moment the sky becomes over-cast, and there are a few species that fly only at dawn and dusk, sleeping for the remainder of the time. Because of this preference for bright sunshine, dragonflies are more common in warm climates. The largest tropical species have a wingspan of up to 10 centimetres (4 inches).

Their legs are grouped well forward on the body and are used to hold their prey, as in a basket. The prey is killed and eaten by means of powerful mandibles, equipped with teeth for both biting and crushing.

The larvae, too, are hunters, and they hunt by an unusual method. The lower lip is hinged and folds back beneath the head. To catch prey, the lip is flicked forward and the victim held by hooks at its end. Dragonfly nymphs are aquatic and, de-pending on the species, the larval stage may last from one to four years or some-times longer. They move well in the water by walking and climbing, or by a kind of jet propulsion in which they draw water into the rectum and expel it forcibly. Most dragonfly nymphs lie in wait for their prey, but there are more aggressive species that stalk potential victims until they are within striking distance of the lower lip.

A lightning attack

The most formidable of all insect predators,
and perhaps the most determined and voracious of all hunters, is the praying mantis. The bodies of mantids have become modified to make them the most specialised of all invertebrate predators.

The front part of the thorax is extended and strengthened. The front pair of legs are very long, armed with curved spines, folded back on themselves like penknives. The mantids are coloured, most commonly green, to harmonise with the plants among which they hide, partly to evade their own enemies and partly to deceive their victims. There are some that run fast in pursuit of prey, but most lie in wait motionless or swaying slightly, head raised and the front legs held out in the attitude of prayer that earned them their name. When threatened they lift themselves still higher and adopt an aggressive attitude, opening the front legs often to display warning coloration.

If the creature that approaches poses no threat, it is assumed to be a victim. The mantis catches it by suddenly extending its front legs which, because of their spines, hold it in a grip from which it cannot escape, while it is torn apart by the insect's man-dibles. The attack is lightning fast, often taking less than 50 milliseconds.

Mantids are aggressive and cannibalistic, so that mating often ends with the male being eaten by the larger female, and once hatched, the larvae must move rapidly out of the reach of their mother.

There are about 1,500 species of mantids, most of which are tropical or sub-tropical, but the name is derived from the most common European species, *Mantis religiosa religiosa.*

Above:
The praying mantis is superbly adapted to its predatory way of life. This one, which lives in the Great Salt Desert of Utah, USA, is camouflaged to match the foliage on which it waits for a victim. Its thorax is long and strong, to extend its reach, and its first pair of legs are positioned well forward. When an insect comes within range these front legs will open and reach forward, then close again, holding the prey firmly between the spines, while the mantis tears it to pieces with its powerful mandibles.

Left:
Perfect camouflage helps this praying mantis, the leaf mimic, to deceive its victims until the last instant.

Cold-blooded killers

The cold-blooded vertebrates are the fishes, amphibians, such as frogs and toads, and the reptiles including the crocodiles and snakes. Many are sophisticated hunters and apart from the lampreys and hagfishes, every group features active carnivores.

Hunters of the sea

Think of fish that hunt, and the first word that springs to mind is 'shark'. Many people think of sharks as tropical fish, but in fact they are common in all seas, except the Antarctic Ocean, and there are about 250 species of them.

A few species will attack humans. The most dangerous are the Great White Shark (*Carcharodon carcharias*), Tiger Shark (*Galeocerdo cuvieri*), Blue Shark (*Prionace*

glauca), Sand or Grey Nurse Shark (*Carcharias taurus*), Hammerhead Shark (*Sphyrna lewini*) and Whaler Shark (*Carcharhinus macrurus*). These are tropical species, but they can occur in high latitudes and the Blue Shark (*P. glauca*) is popular for sea angling. Attacks on humans, however, occur only where the water temperature is between 16° and 21°C, and the sea is rarely this warm north or south of latitude 43°. Most attacks occur during daytime, close inshore, in water 60 centimetres to 1 metre (2 to 3 feet) deep, and therefore to the lower part of the body. The majority of attacks prove fatal, death being due to loss of blood and shock. It seems that sharks are attracted by bright objects at or close to the water surface, and by splashing and noise, like

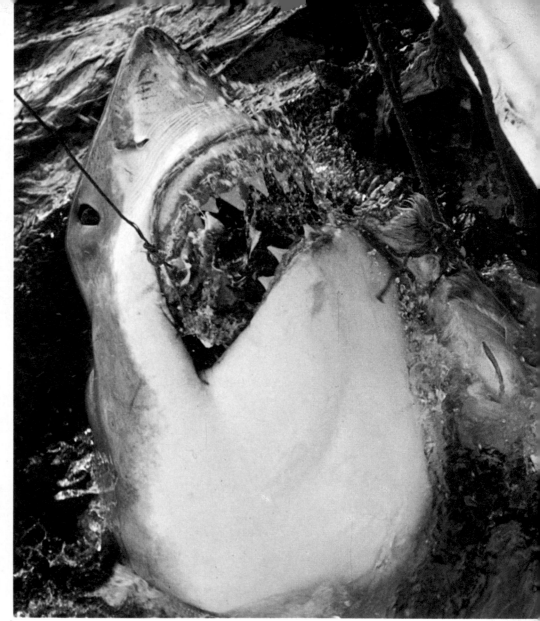

to make a triangular shape. In the Thresher Shark (*Alopius vulpinus*) the caudal fin is much extended.

Sharks have two pairs of strong fins, the pectoral and pelvic; these correspond to limbs in other animals – an anal fin on the underside of the body just in front of the tail, and two dorsal fins on the upper side. Not all sharks are fast swimmers, and the longer and more pointed the fins, the faster the animal can move.

Sharks are not highly manoeuvrable, except for the Bonnet Shark (*Sphyrna tiburo*) and the Hammerhead Shark. In these species the head is greatly widened and flattened, and is used as a rudder.

Apart from the huge Whale Shark (*Rhincodon typus*) which grows to 18 metres (60 feet), and the Basking Shark (*Cetorhinus maximus*) which grows to 12 metres (39 feet), both of which feed on plankton, all the sharks are hunters. They feed on squid, fish and smaller sharks, even of their own species, so that a group of sharks usually consists of individuals all much the same size. All sharks keep out of the way of the most formidable of sharks, the Hammerhead. Within each group there is a well defined hierarchy with individuals feeding in strict order. Sharks do not feed during courtship and breeding, and breeding grounds are selected that are free from

Above:
The teeth of the Great White Shark, like all sharks, have developed from the small spines called denticles which cover the animal's body. They grow continually, and lost teeth are quickly replaced.

Left:
Whaler Sharks hunting in a group. Sharks are attracted by scent and low frequency vibrations, as well as by bright objects near the surface.

that caused by large groups of people. When a shark attacks it selects a victim from which it will not be deterred, so that anyone going to the aid of the victim is unlikely to be attacked.

This fierce predator is not a 'true' fish at all, but a primitive cartilaginous fish whose skeleton is made of cartilage ('gristle') reinforced with bony plates. This is only one of the ways in which sharks differ from bony fish. They are not covered with overlapping scales like true fish, but with plates ending in small spines called denticles; their teeth are also developed from these spines. The teeth are attached to the membrane that covers the inside of the mouth. This grows continually, so that lost teeth are replaced almost immediately. The mouth is on the underside of the body, not at the front. The tail is a continuation of the body, containing the spine, and in most species it curves up slightly to form a long caudal fin, widened by a flap of skin below

larger sharks.

Sharks have an acute sense of smell and locate their prey mainly by scent. Sight is much less important and a shark can only distinguish movement, probably by reflection, but little more. At closer range, pit organs all over the body are used to detect vibrations, and irregular, low frequency vibrations (below 800 Hz) will attract sharks rapidly. Sharks appear suddenly, apparently from nowhere, and often from below their quarry.

They begin the hunt by circling the prey, closing in slowly. As more sharks join the group the impulse to feed is stimulated and the sharks swim more rapidly, which provides a further stimulus. As they move to the attack, the jaws are protruded, which erects the teeth and locks them in position. The bite is powerful. An animal 2.5 metres (8 feet) long may exert a pressure of almost 3 tonnes per square centimetre. Once the prey is gripped by the bite, flesh may be taken by means of vibrating the head or rapid twisting, if the victim is too large to be eaten whole.

Sometimes sharks may be over-stimulated and embark on a frenzy of feeding, in which they will tear at anything, including each other. Probably, this is due to the presence of too many sharks at one time.

The sharks are members of the class Chondrichthyes, the cartilaginous fishes, and their relatives are the skates and rays. In these animals the body has become wide and flat and the pectoral fins have extended forward to the head to form 'wings'. While sharks swim by moving their bodies from side to side, rays swim by moving their pectoral fins up and down, rather like birds flying. The mouth and gill openings are on the underside of the body, the eyes above. Rays are well adapted to life on the sea bottom.

There are about 350 species of rays. They feed on molluscs, crustaceans and small fish, capturing their prey by moving over it and scooping it into their mouths; they often use their fins to do this. Although they are adapted to life at the bottom of the

Right:
The rays are primitive cartilaginous fishes that abandoned vigorous swimming, first to live on the sea bottom, then to move through the water fairly slowly using their large pectoral fins rather like wings. This Electric Ray can stun its prey by delivering a strong electric shock from organs located between the pectoral fins and the head.

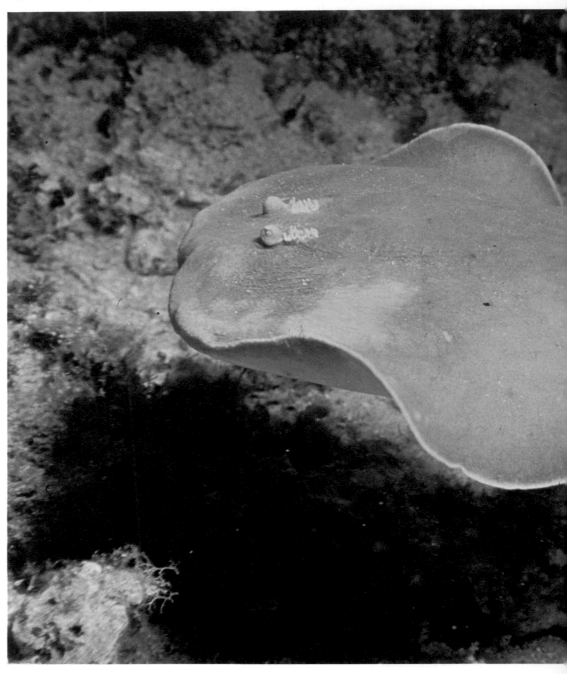

sea, many rays swim in midwater and hunt herring, sprats and other small fish.

The electric rays (family Torpedinidae) have pairs of organs between the pectoral fins and the head that can deliver a powerful electric shock as the animal folds its fins about its prey. The shock stuns the prey, but it is also used in self defence. There are about 20 species of electric rays, of which the most common is the Torpedo (*Torpedo nobiliana*), found all over the North Atlantic. It grows to a length of about 1.5 metres (5 feet) and it is said that its shock can knock down a human who steps on it.

Electric rays have smooth skins, non-electric species have a rough, shark-like skin, often with spines. The stingrays (family Dasyatidae) have a sharp spine at the top of the tail that can inflict severe wounds as the fish lashes its tail, and that injects a poison at the same time. The eagle rays also carry a venomous sting.

The swordfishes, sailfishes and marlins are also formidable hunters of the sea. The

Below:
The upper jaw of this jumping sailfish is lengthened to form a spear for hunting.

Left:
Sailfish can be tiny, as seen here on a human hand.

Bottom:
The sharp spine at the top of this eagle ray's tail carries a venomous sting which injects poison into its prey. Small fish follow to pick up remains of the ray's food.

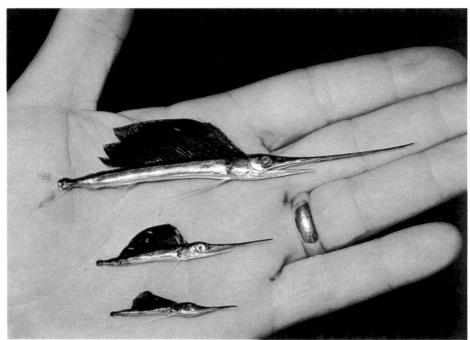

sailfishes (*Istiophorus* species) and marlins
are members of the family Istiophoridae, or
bill-fishes. The upper jaw is lengthened to
form a round spear which is used in hunting, probably to stun prey as the animal
swings its head from side to side. The
sailfishes have a dorsal fin that is much enlarged and which is 'unfurled' when the
fish is relaxing at the surface. When moving
fast it can be folded back into a groove to
improve the streamlining of the body.
Sailfishes are among the fastest of all
swimmers, possibly achieving more than
90 kilometres (60 miles) per hour over short
distances. They are sometimes quite large,
reaching 3 metres (10 feet) or more in
length. The most common species are the
Atlantic (*Istiophorus albicans*) and Pacific
(*I. greyi*) Sailfish. Marlins lack the sail fin.
The largest of them is the Black Marlin
(*Makaira indica*) which grows to more than
4.5 metres (15 feet).

The Swordfish (*Xiphias gladius*) is still
larger, occasionally growing to 6 metres
(19½ feet) or more. Its upper jaw extends
forward to form a horizontally flattened
'sword'.

'Snakes' of the sea

If the fish with swords and spears have a
shape that is useful in hunting, so too, in
quite different ways, have the eels. True
eels are members of the order Apodes,
which means 'without feet'. They are
called this because the pelvic fins are
absent. In many species the dorsal and anal
fins extend to meet around the tail and the
actual tail (caudal fin) appears to be a part
of this continuous fin.

Eels are snake-like, usually without
scales, and their skins are covered in mucus,
which makes them slippery and difficult to
grasp. All eels are carnivorous. The most
common eels, of the genus *Anguilla*, spend
part of their life cycle in fresh water, and
can survive for long periods out of water,
being able to breath through their skin.
They feed on worms and other small animals, and larger specimens will catch and
eat frogs and waterbirds.

The marine species include some that are
much feared by divers and fishermen. The
morays, for example, have large mouths
and strong, sharp teeth and they are very
aggressive, attacking anything they con-
sider to be threatening, or food. They can
inflict severe wounds.

There are about 120 species of morays,
most of them tropical, but there are a few
temperate species, such as the Painted Eel
(*Muraena helena*) which the Romans re-
garded as a great delicacy and kept in ponds,

the Californian Moray (*Gymnothorax mordax*) and the Atlantic Blackedge (*G. nigromarginatus*). Morays have no pectoral fins and the gill openings are reduced to small holes. They range in size from 90 centimetre (3 feet) to 3 metres (10 feet) or more.

Conger eels (*Conger* species) are also large, occasionally growing to 2.5 metres (8 feet) or more, and fiercely predacious.

The eels are bottom feeders, spending their hunting time patrolling the sea, river or lake bed in search of fish or other animals small enough to be seized. The morays are nocturnal, spending the day hiding in crevices.

Other marine eels have evolved into even stranger forms, suitable for a life spent in the cold, dark ocean depths. The snipe eels, for example (family Nemichthyidae) have long, thin jaws like threads, covered in tiny teeth, that are used to entangle their prey. The Bobtail Snipe Eel (*Cyema atrum*) has a short body and long, feather-like tail, but most, like *Nemichthys scolopaceus*, have a long, thin, worm-like body. Snipe eels can swallow animals the same size as themselves. They grow to about 40 centimetres (16 inches) long.

Adaptations to the deep ocean

Life is hard in the deep ocean. The lack of light means there are no green plants to support herbivores. Some animals rise to the surface at night to feed on plankton, others scavenge whatever falls from the water above, and others are predators. Because food is scarce, carnivores must be able to eat large meals whenever there is an opportunity. Many have immense mouths, with a huge gape, and large, sharp teeth.

The gulpers and swallowers have taken this line of development to its limit. The Great, or Black Swallower (*Chiasmodon niger*) is typical. It lives at depths of about 2,500 metres (1½ miles), is up to 15 centimetres (6 inches) long, and is jet black. It consists of a huge mouth and slender body

and tail. It roams the depths and swallows any animal it can catch. It can swallow an animal twice its own size by distending its stomach.

The angler fishes, too, have very large mouths, but they have developed a further aid. The dorsal fin has been modified into a 'rod' on the end of which there is a lure. *Lophius piscatorius* lives on the bottom in shallow, temperate waters, growing to a length of about 45 centimetres (18 inches) and preying on fish of all kinds. There are

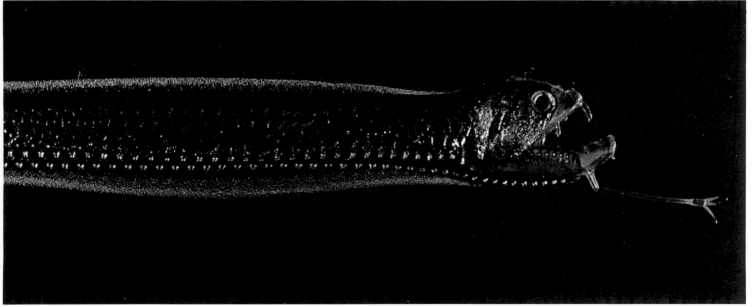

many species of angler fish (order Pediculati), though, and those that live in perpetual darkness often have a lure that is luminous. One of the deepest dwellers is *Melanocetus johnsoni*, found at about 5,500 metres ($3\frac{1}{2}$ miles) below the surface of the Atlantic. *Lasiognathus saccostoma*, which lives at about 3,000 metres ($1\frac{3}{4}$ miles) below the Caribbean, has refined its angling by adding curved hooks to the end of the thin line that bears its luminous lure.

Reproduction can be difficult, too, because individuals are scattered so widely that males and females may seldom meet. The Deep Sea Angler Fish have solved this problem, too. Early in life, while the young still live close together, the males attach themselves to females and become parasites. The two circulatory systems join and as the females grow the males degenerate until they are little more than reproductive organs attached to the females, the bodies completely fused together.

Barracudas – reef hunters

You may never meet an angler fish, but if you visit warm seas you might see a barracuda. The barracudas (family *Sphyraenidae*) hunt in shallower water. There are about 20 species of which the largest, growing to about 180 centimetres (6 feet), is the Pecuda, Becuna, or Great Barracuda (*Sphyraena barracuda*) of Australian waters. Barracudas are solitary animals, lurking around reefs, lying still or moving slowly, ever watchful for any movement. They will approach anything that moves and their attack is fierce and fast. They are voracious and fearless, and they have been known to attack humans.

Barracudas closely resemble pikes, in behaviour as well as appearance. There are not many species of pike and the Common Pike (*Esox lucius*) of northern rivers and lakes is typical. Its large mouth has bands of small teeth on the palate and tongue, and longer teeth in the jaws. These point

Below:
Large barracudas are usually solitary but smaller ones sometimes hunt in shoals, like these, from the Red Sea. Barracudas have been seen to herd shoals of smaller fish into shallow waters from which they cannot escape, holding them there until the barracudas are ready to feed.

backward and can be depressed, allowing prey to enter but not to leave.

Most pike feed on insects and small fish, including other pike, but large ones will take waterbirds and rats.

Like the barracuda, the pike hunts alone, but the gar of North and Central America often hunts in shoals. It feeds so voraciously that its numbers have to be controlled in fishing waters to protect other fish species. The gar is an ancient fish, its body encased in thick, enamelled scales like armour plating, a type of covering that was common in Paleozoic and Mesozoic animals. The species may have survived because the eggs are highly poisonous and so rarely eaten by predators. The jaws of the gar are extended forward to form a beak armed with long rows of needle-like teeth that are very effective at capturing prey. Gars can breathe air and often bask at the surface of the muddy, weedy, shallow rivers in which they live, looking like dead sticks.

The American Gar is a member of the family Lepisosteus, and is not closely related to the fish called gar, garfish or garpike of the Old World, which belongs to the family Belonidae, or needlefishes. These, too, are efficient hunters, having long, slender snouts armed with small but very sharp teeth. The needlefishes live in the sea and swim close to the surface, alone or in groups, hunting the smaller fish on which they feed. They hunt mostly by sight and have large eyes. Many are less than 60 centimetres (2 feet) long, but some species can grow to 1.5 metres (5 feet). They often leap out of the water and occasionally humans in boats are injured when one strikes them.

Above:
The pike is rather like the barracuda, but confined to fresh water, where its mastery of the waters enables it to hover and to stalk its prey. Pikes will eat any small animal, including, as seen here, another pike.

Left:
The needlefishes have jaws that are longer than their heads, equipped with needle-like teeth. They have large eyes and hunt mainly by sight, close to the surface, on such fish as herring and sardines. These are *Xenentodon cancila*, found from India to Malaysia, and are related to flying fish.

Above:
Piranhas are much smaller than their prey, but they are able to bite pieces from an animal of any size. They have powerful jaws, a wide mouth gape, and many sharp, saw-like teeth that cut like scissors.

Above right:
The Red Piranha (*Serrasalmus nattereri*) earns its name from the blood red colour of its belly and fins.

Below:
Archer fish hunt near the water surface, 'shooting down' flying insects with an accurately aimed jet of water.

The Tigerfish (*Hydrocyon* species) of Africa, which grow up to 1 metre (approx 3 feet) long, also resemble pike, and are perhaps fiercer. They are members of the family Characidae, whose most notorious members are the South American piranhas (*Serrasalmus* species). Piranhas are deep-bodied fish. They live in large shoals and will attack any animal, of any size, that ventures into the water.

If piranhas are spectacular hunters, perhaps the most remarkable of all fresh water carnivorous fish is *Toxotes jaculator*, the Archer Fish of Malaysia and Java. In the wild, the archer fish grows to a length of about 12 centimetres (5 inches), but some-

times if they are kept in tanks they can grow to about 18 centimetres (7 inches) *T. jaculator* is the best known of several species of archer fish. What all of them share in common is the method by which they catch their prey. They live on insects, which they shoot out of the air by ejecting a jet of water. *T. jaculator* can throw its jet as much as 180 centimetres (nearly 6 feet), and with great accuracy. Once it is wetted the insect falls to the waiting fish.

If fish have evolved more ways of finding food than other classes of animal, it is because the class Osteichthyes, the bony fishes, contains more species than any other vertebrate class. There are at least 30,000 species of bony fish.

Amphibians

The amphibians, including frogs, toads, salamanders and newts are the most primitive of the land-dwelling vertebrates, and were the first to leave the water. Some still spend much of their lives in water. Amphibians lose water from their bodies easily, so they are not common in dry places, and no modern amphibian can tolerate salt water. Despite this, frogs have colonised many remote islands, which they must have reached by riding on floating vegetation.

Most frogs and toads begin life as herbivorous tadpoles and end this stage with a

long fast, during which their adult jaws develop and they are nourished by absorbing their own tails. Most adult forms are carnivorous. They have teeth only in the upper jaw and their very long tongues are attached at the front of the mouth, are deeply cleft at the tip, and are covered with a sticky substance. They eat mainly insects, which they catch in flight with their tongues, but larger species eat animals such as snails, worms, small fish and other amphibians. The largest of all frogs is the Goliath Frog (*Rana goliath*) which lives in Africa. It can grow to a length of 90 centimetres (35½ inches) and is capable of swallowing a rat. When eating large prey, the food is helped into the mouth by the fore limbs. Some species are voracious eaters, and tend to stay in such a small feeding area, that they are popular as destroyers of farm and garden pests.

Females are always larger than males, and only males are vocal. The Common Frog of Europe and Asia (*Rana temporaria*) and its American cousin *R. sylvatica* are the only amphibians that live inside the Arctic Circle.

There is no clear distinction between frogs and toads, and the difference between a newt and a salamander is only that the newt is smaller. The salamanders include the largest of all living amphibians, the Japanese Giant Salamander (*Andria*

japonicus) which reaches a length of 1.5 metres (5 feet) or more. It lives its entire life in water, eating fish, worms, crabs and anything else it can catch by swimming or walking on the bottom.

Amphibians have adapted to many ways of life. The frog family Leptodactylidae dig deep burrows and the tree frogs (family Hylidae) live in trees. Perhaps the most extraordinary adaptation of all, however, is found in the Axolotl (*Ambystoma mexicanum*). It reaches sexual maturity while still a larva, and it remains a larva throughout its life unless it should find itself in a dry habitat. When this happens it loses its gills and becomes a typical salamander.

Top:
The Corroboree frog of New South Wales, Australia, breeds in sphagnum moss and feeds on insects, which it catches on the end of its long, sticky tongue.

Above:
Like many salamanders the Fire, or Spotted Salamander (*Salamandra salamandra*) escapes from its enemies by wriggling on its belly – in effect, by swimming on land. This one is about to catch an earthworm.

51

Reptiles

Although reptiles and amphibians are cold-
blooded vertebrates, and both are descended from fishes, reptiles are the most
advanced of the three. Having scales that
prevent the loss of water through the skin,
they can live in dry places, and they are
fully adapted to life on land.

The largest and most impressive of the
modern reptiles are the members of the
order Crocodylia, which includes the
families Crocodylidae (crocodiles), Alli-
gatoridae (alligators and caimans) and
Gavialidae (gavial).

There is only one species of Gavial, or
Gharial, *Gavialis gangeticus*. It lives in the
rivers of India and differs from other
crocodilians in having a longer, more
slender snout and 27 to 29 teeth in each
jaw, compared with 22 or less in other
members of the order. The gavial grows to a
length of 3.5 to 4.5 metres (11½ to 14½ feet),
it is an underwater hunter and feeds mainly
on fish, which it catches by swinging its
head horizontally.

Alligators and caimans have broader
snouts than crocodiles, but the main difference between the families is in their teeth.

Left:
A crocodile will kill small animals with a single bite, but to kill larger animals, like this impala, it must drag them below the surface of the water and hold them until they drown.

Below:
If the crocodile's prey is too large to swallow in one piece a difficulty arises. The hunter is unable to bite off pieces and it cannot pull at pieces either, for it is in the water and there is no fixed object against which it can gain a purchase. It solves the problem by gripping a limb tightly, then spinning rapidly on its own axis, literally twisting off pieces of food.

Those in the lower jaw of alligators fit inside those of the upper jaw when the mouth is closed, while in crocodiles the teeth of both jaws interlock to form a single row of alternately upper and lower teeth. Both families have a large fourth tooth in each side of the lower jaw. When an alligator closes its mouth this tooth fits into a recess in the upper jaw and is concealed. When a crocodile closes its mouth the fourth tooth is exposed. If you find yourself looking at a crocodilian with its mouth closed, and you can see this large fourth tooth, then the animal is a crocodile.

All crocodilians live in much the same way. They never move very far from water and all of them are strong swimmers. The nostrils and eyes are on top of the crocodile's head, so that when it floats in the water only its eyes and nostrils are exposed; it then looks very like a dead log. The nostrils open into bony tubes that end behind the throat valve, so it can swallow and breathe simultaneously and cannot drown by inhaling water through the mouth. It feeds on any animal it can catch and will capture and eat prey larger than itself if the opportunity occurs.

Crocodile attack

The crocodile lies in the water, waiting. When an animal enters the water it moves towards it slowly, submerging with barely a ripple and swimming beneath the surface. The attack is launched when it is within about 6 metres (19½ feet), by a few powerful strokes of the tail which carry it the last short distance at great speed. The prey is seized and either killed at once by the first bite or pulled beneath the surface to drown.

A crocodilian cannot chew its food and if it is too large to be swallowed whole, it is broken into pieces by being held firmly while the crocodilian spins rapidly on its own axis to twist off a piece. The thrashing that is seen when a crocodile or alligator captures a large animal is not caused by the struggles of the victim, but by the hunter eating its quarry, whose death was quick and clean.

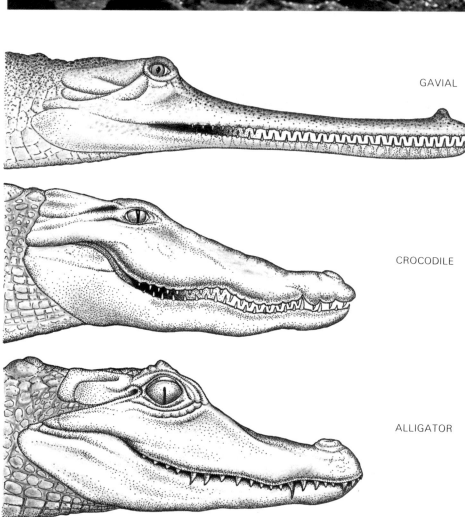

GAVIAL

CROCODILE

ALLIGATOR

Right:
When it is on land you can see the ways in which caimans are adapted to aquatic hunting. The eyes and nostrils are on top of the head. The digits on the hind feet are webbed. The tail is flattened and broadened for swimming and the colour of the animal is very similar that of the water, and the banks from which it hunts. This caiman lives in Amazonia, South America.

Below:
The chameleon, like many lizards, has layers of skin containing pigments that it uses to make its own colour match that of the vegetation on which it waits for its prey. This chameleon is green and brown while it sits on a branch surrounded by leaves, but it becomes progressively more green as it moves deeper into the foliage.

Caimans rarely exceed 2 metres ($6\frac{1}{2}$ feet) in length and while this makes them the smallest of the modern crocodilians, the size of these animals is often exaggerated. The largest is little more than 6 metres ($19\frac{1}{2}$ feet) and most crocodiles and alligators are not much more than half that length. Few will attack humans. The Nile Crocodile (*Crocodylus niloticus*) and the Salt-water, or Estuarine Crocodile (*C. porosus*) do so occasionally, and all large crocodilians are dangerous, but like most predators, they seldom attack animals they do not intend to eat, unless in self-defence.

Turtles

Most people assume that turtles are all vegetarians. This is quite untrue and it may be one reason why so many pets die from want of proper attention. None can chew tough, fibrous plant material, most are omnivores, and some are carnivores. The Central European Pond Tortoise (*Emys orbicularis*), for example, feeds on insects, frogs and tadpoles, and fish – and some large aquatic turtles eat birds and small mammals.

The Common Snapper (*Chelydra serpentina*) and Alligator Snapper (*Macrochelys temminckii*) of North America are large and aggressive, inflicting severe bites on any human that comes too close. The Alligator Snapper spends much of its time lying on the river bottom, looking exactly like a stone covered with weeds. When it opens its mouth it reveals two white growths that look like worms. Fish are attracted to these and may approach, so entering the turtle's mouth.

Not all turtles have hard shells. Among the more than 200 species of Chelonia, about 20 are soft-shelled species belonging to the family Trionychidae. They feed on fishes, frogs and molluscs and are strictly aquatic.

Some lizards look like newts, others like small crocodiles. In fact, they are quite different from both. They are members of the reptilian order Squamata, which also

includes the snakes, to which lizards are
closely related. There may be as many as
3,000 species of lizards and they have
adapted to almost every terrestrial environment, although none is completely
aquatic and only a few can live close to the
Arctic Circle. Most have a long, slim body,
a long tail and four limbs, but there is much
variation. Their teeth are usually simple,
like pegs. There are some herbivorous
lizards, such as the iguanas and agamas, but
most are carnivores, the smaller ones feeding largely on insects.

Venomous lizards

There are only two species of venomous
lizard, the Gila Monster (*Heloderma sus-
pectum*) and the Beaded Lizard (*H. horri-
dum*), and both live in south-west USA and
Mexico. They hunt smaller lizards and
rodents and their bite, though unpleasant,
is rarely fatal to humans. The chameleons
have sticky tongues half as long as their
bodies, which they shoot out to capture any
insect within reach. In common with such
lizards as the American anole (*Anolis*
species) and Asiatic bloodsuckers (*Calotes*
species) chameleons can match their body
colour to that of their surroundings as a
method of concealment from both their
enemies and their prey.

Chameleons live in trees and have toes
adapted for gripping, and prehensile tails,
while geckos are often found in houses.
Most have adhesive pads on their toes and
those of the genus *Lygodactylus* on the tail
as well to enable them to climb walls. Many
geckos are nocturnal, unlike the majority of
lizards which like warm sunshine. The flying dragons (*Draco* species) of Malaysia are
able to glide by means of extensions of skin
on their flanks, held by elongated ribs.

The largest lizards are the monitors

(family Varanidae). There are 24 species, found in many of the warm parts of the Old World. The largest of all is the Komodo Dragon (*Varanus komodoensis*), which grows to about 3 metres (10 feet) and feeds mainly on small pigs, but will eat almost anything else it can find. It hunts by day and can chase its prey, running at about 16 kilometres (10 miles) per hour.

You can distinguish most lizards from snakes because they have legs, but there are more than 150 species of legless lizards. The Common Slow-worm (*Anguis fragilis*), popular with gardeners because it eats slugs, is a lizard that looks like a snake, as is the much larger Glass Snake (*Ophisaurus apodus*) of southern Europe, which grows to well over one metre.

Snakes – sophisticated killers

There are about 3,000 species of snakes, found in most parts of the world apart from the Arctic and Antarctic and some islands, most notably Ireland. They range in size from thread snakes (family Leptotyphlopidae) some of which are no more than 10 centimetres (4 inches) long to the Reticulated Python (*Python reticulatus*) which grows to 9 metres ($29\frac{1}{2}$ feet) or more.

All snakes hunt. The blind snakes, thread snakes and anomalepid snakes are blind, burrowing animals that live on termites and other small invertebrates. The larger burrowing snakes include some that are brightly coloured, like *Anilius scytale*, a South American species that is banded in red and black, like some coral snakes. The

Left:
Pythons are large snakes that have no venom, they kill by constriction. This Indian Python can grow to 6.5 metres (21 feet) long and snakes of this size have been known to swallow prey the size of a small deer or leopard, but pythons generally take smaller prey.

Below:
The Old World true lizards often fall victim to larger predators such as snakes, but they are not defenceless. This Green Lizard (*Lacerta viridis*) is attacking an Asp Viper (*Vipera aspis*), a southern European snake not to be confused with the Egyptian asp.

larger snakes eat eels and other snakes, and *A. scytale* belongs to a family (Aniliidae) all of whose members have vestiges of hind limbs in the shape of small claws near the base of the tail.

The boas, pythons and wood snakes (family Boidae) also have these claws near the tail. They are non-poisonous and kill their prey by constriction, winding coils of their bodies around the victim and so causing suffocation. They do not crush the victim.

The venomous snakes fall into three families. The Viperidae include the asps, adders, vipers, rattlesnakes, copperheads and moccasins. All of them have very long fangs. When the snake closes its mouth the fangs fold back into a recess in the roof of

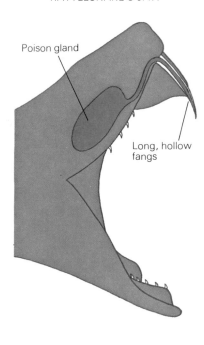

Poison gland

Long, hollow fangs

the mouth. When the mouth is opened they are extended and point forward. Vipers stab their prey with these fangs, injecting venom, which flows down grooves in the fangs. They then pursue their prey until it dies.

The Elapidae have much shorter fangs, so they must bite their victims in order to inject venom. This family includes the cobras, mambas, coral snakes, venomous sea snakes, kraits and the Australian Taipan (*Oxyuranus scutellatus*), said to be the world's most venomous snake.

The Colubridae includes the majority of snakes, including grass snakes, smooth snakes, house snakes, the Indian Flying Snake (*Chrysopelea ornata*) and the Boomslang (*Dispholidus typus*). Only some are venomous and few of those are dangerous to large mammals because their fangs are located far back in the jaw and are small. There are exceptions, however. The Boomslang can be dangerous.

Prey swallowed whole

Lacking limbs and having teeth designed to seize and hold prey but not to cut or chew, snakes have to swallow animals whole and a snake can swallow an animal larger than its own head. The upper and lower jaws are connected by elastic ligaments, giving the snake a very large gape. The left and right sides of the lower jaw can be moved a little way back and forth independently of one another. Prey is usually swallowed head first and as soon as the head is in the snake's mouth it is held by the upper teeth on one side while the lower jaw on the opposite side moves forward, grips the food and draws it back, swinging it around the upper teeth that hold it. It is then held on the other side and the motion is repeated, the food being 'walked' into the mouth until it can be swallowed, the body distending to accommodate it. The process sometimes breaks a few teeth, but the snake grows teeth constantly.

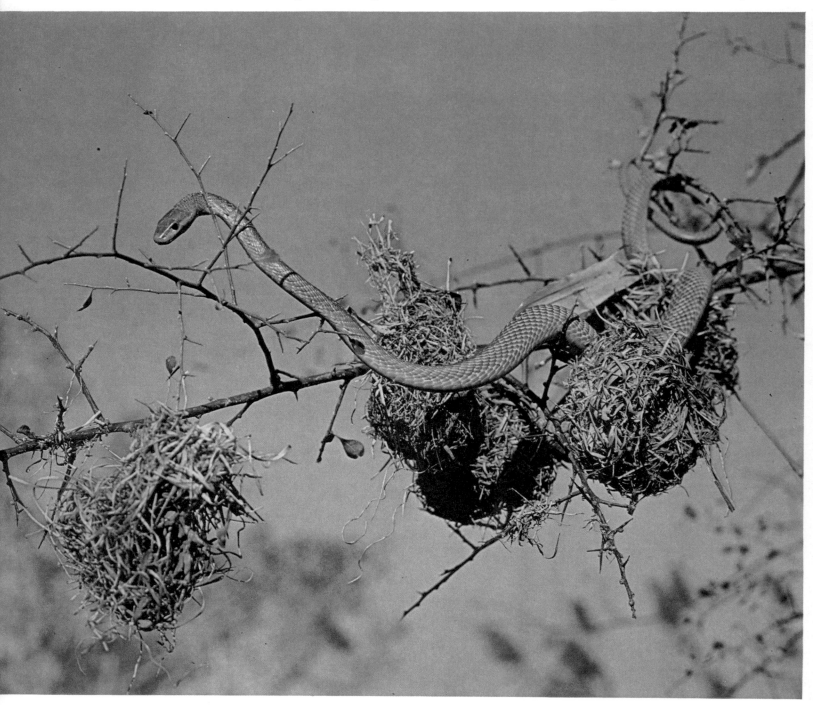

The technique of eating is very highly developed in the African Egg-eating Snake (*Dasypeltis scaber*) which has few teeth and which swallows eggs intact. A bony projection from the backbone into the gullet cuts through the shell, the liquid is swallowed and the shell removed by vomiting.

Snakes hunt by sight and smell. They use their forked tongues to collect particles from the air which are then carried to a chemo-receptor, in the roof of the mouth. Some species are sensitive to heat. By detecting an object that is slightly warmer than their surroundings, snakes such as the pit vipers can hunt by night.

Each year about 30,000 people die from snakebites, yet most snakes are not aggressive toward animals that are too large for them to eat, and they will not attack unless threatened. Many of their threatening gestures, such as hissing, expanding hoods in cobras and rattling tails in rattlesnakes are defensive.

Snakes play an important part in controlling the numbers of rodents and other animals that farmers regard as vermin.

Above:
When threatened, many snakes seek to deter aggressors by making themselves look larger and more dangerous than they are. The Small Spotted Coral Snake (*Calliophis maculiceps*) displays the underside of its tail, coloured white, red and black; colours which are often associated with a disagreeable taste.

Inset:
The Cobra makes itself larger by widening its body just behind its head, giving it the famous 'hood'. This, too, is a defensive posture.

Left:
The egg-eating snakes are highly specialised feeders, eating eggs of all kinds but nothing else.

Opposite top:
When the snake closes its mouth the fangs fold back out of the way. When it strikes the snake need only inflict one stab, which is sufficient to inject a dose of poison. The rattlesnake is one of the most efficient of all reptilian hunters.

Opposite bottom:
Green mambas live in trees and are found in the forests of Africa. They are large snakes, growing to 2 metres (6½ feet) or more in length and, like all mambas, their venom is a powerful nerve poison.

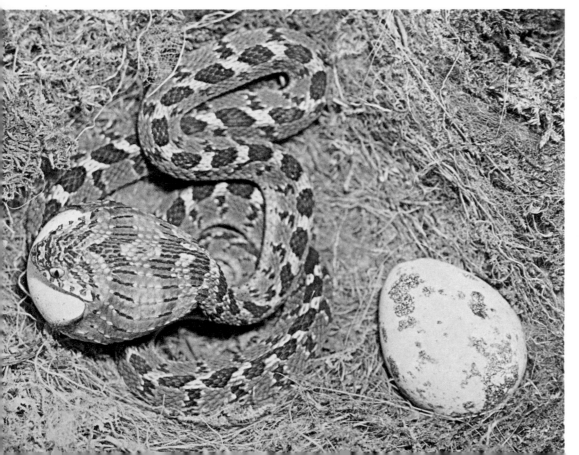

59

Hunters of the air

Birds and mammals are descended from reptiles but differ from them in being warm-blooded. This means they can control the temperature of their bodies and so lead an active life in climates that are too cold for reptiles or amphibians. To do this, however, they require much more food.

Fishers of the shoreline

Walk along any beach or beside the sandbanks or mudflats of a tidal river, and you will see many birds with long legs and bills. They are waders, members of the order Charadriiformes, and they include the families of the oystercatchers, plovers, snipes, avocets, phalaropes, pratincoles and stone curlews.

Waders are hunters. Their long legs and bills enable them to enter the water and to delve into the sand or mud. They vary greatly in size. The Common Turnstone (*Arenaria interpres*) is only about 23 centimetres (9 inches) long. It seeks its diet of insects, molluscs and small crustaceans in the intertidal zone, rummaging among seaweed and turning over stones; a habit that accounts for its name. It is an Arctic bird that is sometimes seen in the far north of Europe or America. The Eurasian Curlew (*Numenius arquata*), on the other hand, is about 56 centimetres (22 inches) long and the largest of European waders. It is easily recognised by its long, downward curving bill. Curlews often gather in large flocks.

The animals hunted by waders hide themselves in burrows in the sand or mud, so the length of a bird's bill determines which animals it can reach to eat. The Ringed Plover (*Charadrius hiaticula*), a small bird 19 centimetres (7½ inches) long with a short bill can reach cockles but a bill the length of the curlew's is needed to reach a ragworm.

The Common or Pied Oystercatcher (*Haemotopos ostralegus*) is one of the showiest of the waders. It occurs in only a few places in North America, but is common all around the coasts of western Europe, especially in the north, where it lives in noisy, excitable flocks. It is about 43 centimetres (17 inches) long, black and white, has a bright orange bill and legs, and feeds on such small marine animals as it can find among the rocks and in the mud and sand.

Many waders have bills designed for probing in search of hidden food, but the oystercatcher does not probe. It has its own distinctive way of eating bivalve shellfish. It waits patiently until the shellfish opens its valves slightly, then stabs at the hinge muscles, so opening the valves fully and revealing the occupant.

The commonest British shore-bird is the tiny Dunlin (*Calidris alpina*), about 18 centimetres (7 inches) long. It occurs all round the west and north of Britain, in western Ireland, and around much of the coast of North America. In Europe it sometimes travels in flocks to inland waters. Its long, slightly downward-curved bill is used to catch small animals and insects.

Insectivorous birds

Although a shore-bird, the pratincole has taken to hunting insects in the air, rather than living as a wader. To catch insects in flight a bird must be a strong flier, fast and manoeuvrable.

The most aerial of all birds are the swifts (family Apodidae). They mate and bathe on the wing and alight only to cling to vertical surfaces. The European Common Swift (*Apus apus*), which winters in Africa, and the North American Chimney Swift (*Chaetura pelagica*) which winters in the upper Amazon region, are two of the most common of the 76 species. Some Asiatic swifts (*Collocalia* species) make nests that are the main ingredient of bird's nest soup.

The swifts are related to hummingbirds, members of the order Apodiformes and are not related to the swallows and martins with which they are sometimes confused. Members of the swallow family (Hirudinidae) are perching birds, but they, too, catch insects in flight. The Common, or Barn Swallow (*Hirundo rustica*), which occurs as a summer visitor all over the nor-

Top left:
Plovers are shore-birds which feed by snapping up any small invertebrate animals they find as they run along. The short, straight bill is also used for probing into sand and mud.

Above left:
The Common Snipe (*Gallinago gallinago*) is about the size of a thrush and feeds on the shore or in shallow water, where its long, straight bill is used to probe in the sand or mud for invertebrates.

Left:
The Curlew (*Numenius arquata*) uses its long, curved bill to probe for worms and other invertebrates that live in fairly deep burrows along the shore.

Below:
The Swift (*Apus apus*) is one of the most aerial of birds and feeds on insects it catches in flight. Its legs allow it to alight, but not to move about on the ground. Its small bill has a wide gape.

thern hemisphere, can be distinguished from its relatives the martins by its long forked tail with streamers.

Hunting for insects in flight has earned the flycatchers their common name. The most common Old World species are the Spotted Flycatcher (*Muscicapa striata*) and the Pied Flycatcher (*Ficedula hypoleuca*). They are small birds, 12 to 15 centimetres (4½ to 6 inches) long, and members of the same family as thrushes and warblers (Muscicapidae). The North American flycatchers are quite different birds. They are quarrelsome and very ready to fight, a trait that gives the family its name of tyrant flycatcher (Tyrannidae). Most are tropical. There are more than 400 species of Old World flycatchers and more than 350 New World species.

The European Bee-eater (*Merops apiaster*) is also named after the food it eats, although its diet is not confined to bees but includes butterflies and dragonflies, all caught on the wing. It is a handsome bird, about 28 centimetres (11 inches) long, vividly coloured in chestnut and yellow above and blue-green below, and with a long, curved bill.

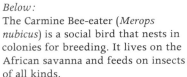

Below:
The Carmine Bee-eater (*Merops nubicus*) is a social bird that nests in colonies for breeding. It lives on the African savanna and feeds on insects of all kinds.

Adaptations to diet

Birds that catch insects may do so either by picking them from plants or from a solid surface, or they may catch them in flight. The bill that is useful for one method may not serve for the other. Many songbirds, like the Song Thrush (*Turdus philomelos*) and Blackbird (*T. merula*) have a varied diet that includes berries, fruit, earthworms, slugs, snails and insects. Their bills are long, slender, sharp, but robust. They are used with great precision to probe the top few centimetres of soil and to hold securely the worm that is half buried and trying to escape. The swallow, on the other hand, has a short bill, but a very wide mouth gape. It does not pick at its prey, but opens its mouth to form the widest cavern possible and gathers insects as it flies through their swarms.

The legs and feet, too, reflect different modes of feeding. The thrushes, including the Blackbird, spend a lot of time seeking food close to the ground, so they have large, strong feet and legs. The swallow has very small, weak feet and legs that are useless for walking and are used only for perching.

It is not necessary for a bird to catch its

insect food in flight. The woodpeckers find insects and their larvae in decaying wood. Woodpeckers have short legs and strong, curved claws to help them climb trees. Their stiff tail feathers provide a firm support when they are hacking into trees and their bills are built like chisels for chipping away the bark. Long, thin tongues with barbs at the tips extract wood-boring grubs from their burrows. To prevent wood chips from entering their nostrils woodpeckers have feathers that cover the upper part of their bills.

The woodpeckers are members of an order (Piciformes) that includes the toucans and other tropical birds. There are about 180 species of woodpeckers found all over the world except in Australasia. The Greater Spotted Woodpecker (*Dendrocopos major*) is probably the most widespread Old World species and is closely related to the American Downy Woodpecker (*D. pubescens*).

Woodpeckers are highly adapted to life spent in the trees, but the Green Woodpecker (*Picus viridis*) is one of several species that spends part of its time hunting for insects on open ground.

Above:
It is not certain why toucans, such as this Laminated Toucan (*Andigena Laminirostris*) have such spectacular bills. They may be used to reach fruit or to intimidate other birds, or in display. Toucans live in the forests of South America and although most feed on fruit, some eat large insects, the nestlings of other birds, and snakes.

Left:
The Spotted Flycatcher might be mistaken for a sparrow, but it is a member of the thrush family and feeds on berries and insects caught in flight.

The fishers

It is easy to imagine that the relationship between a predator and its prey is a simple one, concerning only the species that eats and the one that is eaten. However, this is not always the case. There are occasions when a third species is involved. In the hot climates of southern Europe, Africa and Asia, cattle are greatly troubled by ticks and other parasites. There are several species of birds that feed on these parasites, these birds live with the animals and spend most of their time perched on their backs. This kind of relationship is called *mutualism*, where two different species of animal live together to the benefit of both. In this example, the birds obtain food, and the cattle are relieved of irritating pests.

One bird that feeds in this way, mainly on the backs of water buffalo, is the Cattle Egret (*Ardeola ibis*), a white bird about 50 centimetres (19½ inches) long with buff coloured feathers on its head and back. It has established itself in North America and parts of South America, too, having moved there between the 1940s and '60s. Another name for this bird is the Buff-backed Heron and this gives us a clue to its true identity. It is a member of the suborder Ardeidae, the family of the herons, bitterns and egrets.

Most of the herons and their relatives feed on fish, supplemented with amphibians, molluscs and insects. They stand motionless in or beside the water for long

periods, waiting for a victim to come within reach, when it is seized with their long, sharp bill. The most common European heron is the Grey Heron (*Ardea cinerea*), a bird about 90 centimetres (19½ inches) long. Its North American equivalent, the Great Blue Heron (*A. herodias*) is larger, reaching about 130 centimetres (51 inches).

The White Stork (*Ciconia ciconia*), has legendary fame for standing on one leg and bringing babies and good luck, yet it is a formidable fish hunter and, at about 100 centimetres (39 inches), larger than the Grey Heron.

The pelicans are no less famous, for their huge bills with elastic pouches in which they scoop up, but do not store, their fish. During hot weather they let their young shelter in the pouch.

Pelicans look clumsy on land but they fly strongly and gracefully. Pelicans belong to the order Pelecaniformes, which also includes other fish-eating birds such as the cormorants, gannets and frigate-birds.

Some of these are strong swimmers, but the bird most adapted to life in the water is the penguin. There are 18 species in the penguin family (Spheniscidae) and they comprise a complete order (Sphenisci-formes) which means they have no close relatives. They are confined to the southern hemisphere, but do not live only in the Antarctic: there are penguins at the Equator, too.

Their feathers are narrow and like scales and their wing bones are flattened to make paddles and cannot be folded like those of other birds. The legs are covered by the skin of the body and the feet are set far back, so that the bird walks on land only with difficulty. In the water, however, a penguin swims as easily and as gracefully as a small seal, propelling itself with its paddle-wings and using its feet as a rudder. If it is in a hurry, it will move in this way on land, too.

Penguins spend most of their time in the water, sometimes swimming with just their heads above the surface, sometimes diving and surfacing repeatedly, like porpoises.

Opposite top:
The Cattle Egret serves this buffalo by removing the parasitic ticks and flies that trouble all cattle. The buffalo serves the bird by allowing it to feed unmolested on its back.
Opposite bottom:
The Green Heron (*Butorides virescens*) waits motionless for prey to come within range then uses its powerful bill to seize and hold its victim.
Top:
Penguins swim under water as easily and gracefully as a seal.
Above:
These Brown Pelicans are competing for a fish one of them has caught. The bill and pouch is used like a scoop to net fish.

They often swim below the surface, with top speeds of about 40 kilometres (25 miles) per hour, in pursuit of fish. They feed on crustaceans, squid and vertebrate fish.

The snake-eaters

The darters (*Anhinga* species) are also strong swimmers, hunting in large rivers and lakes in many of the warmer parts of the world. They look like cormorants, but have much longer necks and long, pointed bills with serrated edges to ensure that once caught, a slippery victim cannot escape. They are members of the pelican order (Pelecaniformes) and despite their other common name of 'snakebird', they do not eat snakes, the name being derived from their serpentine necks, with which they strike at their prey.

Many birds do eat snakes however, and although great size can protect a snake (or any other animal) from attack by birds, venom cannot. Snake venom is seldom dangerous if swallowed and birds are too quick to risk being bitten.

The White Stork augments its fish diet with snakes and lizards and so do some kingfishers. The Common European Kingfisher (*Alcedo atthis*) is no more than 16 centimetres ($6\frac{1}{4}$ inches) long, but most members of the kingfisher family (Alcedinidae) are tropical and some are much larger and hunt on land rather than in and beside water.

The largest of all the kingfishers is the Australian Kookaburra, or Laughing Jackass (*Dacelo novaeguinae*), which is three times the size of its European relative. It has a habit of sitting silently for a long time and then, most commonly at dawn and dusk, embarking on a long duet with another Kookaburra, their 'song' sounding very like human laughter. It catches reptiles of all kinds, including venomous species, banging them on the ground until they are dead. This behaviour is probably

Below:
The Kookaburra, or Laughing Jackass, is the largest of all kingfishers and lives in Australia. This one has caught a snake, which it will hold in its strong bill and kill by beating it repeatedly on the ground or against the tree.

Below right:
Snakes form an important part of the Yellow-billed Hornbill's diet and it hunts for them on the ground.

instinctive, since any piece of butcher's meat a Kookaburra obtains will be treated in the same way.

The kingfishers are members of the same order (Coraciiformes) as the Bucerotidae, or hornbills, birds whose bills are surmounted by large, horny protuberances, often brightly coloured. The hornbills live in the Old World tropics and while most live in trees and feed on fruit and insects, there are other species that dwell on the ground and hunt for larger animals. Poisonous animals make up a substantial part of the diet of some Asiatic hornbills, and there are species that will work together as a group to kill a snake that is too large for a single bird to tackle. The largest of the hornbills is the Great Indian Two-horned Hornbill (*Buceros bicornis*) which is about 1.5 metres (5 feet) long.

The most remarkable characteristic of all the hornbills, however, is their habit of walling up the female in a hollow tree while she incubates the eggs and raises the young to an age at which they can fly. During this time she is fed by the male through a small hole in the mud wall behind which she is sealed.

The most fearsome hunter of snakes is the Secretary Bird (*Sagittarius serpentes*) which stands about 120 centimetres (almost 4 foot) tall, It has 10 long feathers behind its head that look very like quill pens held behind the ear of the 18th century office clerk, and it is easy to see how it earned its name from the first European naturalists to find it in central, eastern and southern Africa. It looks dignified, slightly comic, but also menacing. It spends most of its time on the ground, although it can fly strongly. A Secretary Bird can walk faster than a man can run. It roosts in trees at night, flying down in the morning to stalk carefully through short grass (it does not like long grass) inspecting the ground and striking suddenly at any small animal it

Left:
The Belted Kingfisher (*Megaceryle alcyon*) lives entirely on fish, which it catches by diving into the water and kills by beating them against a branch before swallowing them whole. When under water its eyes are protected by a membrane.

Below:
The African Secretary Bird prefers to hunt in short grass, stalking carefully in search of small mammals and reptiles. The most venomous of snakes has little chance against this powerful hunter.

Right:
The African River Eagle attacks at high speed, at the last moment extending its legs forward so it can seize its prey in its powerful talons. Its keen eyesight enables it to see fish just below the surface of the water.

Far right:
The sea eagles can be distinguished from the true eagles by their naked lower legs. The Bald Eagle, emblem of the United States, is a typical sea eagle and a close relative of the African River Eagle. It is not bald, but has white feathers on its head and neck which give it its name.

sees. Its weapons are its fierce talons and its speed. It strikes and jumps back far too quickly for any snake to strike it and it strikes again and again until the prey is dead. Secretary Birds are sometimes tamed and kept on farms to kill snakes and rodents.

Kings of the air

The Secretary Bird is the only surviving member of its family (Sagittariidae) and so it has no close relatives. However its strong, hooked bill and talons show that it is a bird of prey, a member of the order Falconiformes, together with the hawks, eagles, falcons and vultures.

These birds are the kings of the air and most of them will capture reptiles, like their distant relative, the Secretary Bird. Indeed, there are eagles that *prefer* a diet of snakes. A few eagles, like the African Tawny Eagle (*Aquila rapax*) and the vultures feed mainly on carrion, but most Falconiformes are predators. The Golden Eagle (*Aquila chrysaetos*) can attack at speeds sometimes in excess of 160 kilometres (100 miles) per hour.

These birds of prey are famed for their soaring and hovering flight, the skill that demonstrates in such a spectacular fashion their total mastery of the air.

Flight by something heavier than air is impossible unless air moves across an aerofoil surface to produce lift. The amount of lift produced depends on the speed of the airflow and on the shape and attitude of the aerofoil surfaces; different shapes and angles of attack with regard to the airflow, being best suited to different flying speeds. The falconiform birds can face into the wind, hold their wings at the angle that reduces their stalling speed to its lowest possible value, sometimes by moving feathers to change their shape, and so glide forward at a speed exactly equal to that of the wind. Their airspeed equals the wind-speed, but since they are travelling in the opposite direction they are stationary in relation to the ground. Soaring flight is achieved by seeking upcurrents in the same way as a glider pilot, but with much greater sensitivity. Neither soaring nor hovering are possible in still air, but a bird of prey can glide in circles, losing height only very slowly.

They have keen eyesight, and can observe small animals far below them even if they are partly concealed by vegetation.

They have forward vision, which enables them to judge distances accurately.

The bill is short, strong and has an upper mandible that curves down and over the lower mandible, ending in a sharp point. The gape of the mouth is very wide. The bill is used only to tear food into pieces small enough to be swallowed whole. It is not a weapon of attack or defence. It is the claws that are used to seize and hold prey and to defend the bird against its own enemies, although birds of prey are less adept at self-defence than they may seem. All four toes have strong, curved talons, although the carrion-eating vultures, which do not need to seize and carry off their food, have much shorter, blunter talons than the hunters.

When a bird is in flight, it is not always easy to tell one member of the order from another, but there are a few general rules that help. Vultures are very large, have broad wings, usually square-tipped and with a straight leading edge. Their tails are short and in most species the head is naked. Eagles have similar wings but their heads are very prominent and the large bill is often clearly visible. Buzzards look like eagles but have much broader tails. Har-

riers have long, narrow wings, often held in a shallow V-shape, and the tips of the primary feathers are usually visible, looking rather like fingers at the wing tips. They have long, narrow, square-tipped tails. Kites are very similar, but larger, and have a distinct fork in the tail. Hawks have broad, rounded wings with the tips of the primaries visible, and long, straight tails. Falcons have pointed wings and long tails.

Below:
Vultures and hyenas sharing a meal of an animal the hyenas probably killed. Close relatives of the eagles, the Old World vultures eat only carrion and have shorter, blunter talons than eagles since they do not need to seize and carry prey.

Golden Eagle, have feathers growing down their legs to the feet, which look like boots. There are about eight races of Golden Eagles living in different parts of the world and at one time the kings of Europe used them to hunt game.

Like all the birds of prey, they mate for life and return year after year to the same nest, built in a high tree or on a cliff. The nest is always built in a place that is inaccessible except from the air. This is necessary, because the family is at its most vulnerable while the eggs are being incubated and the young reared to an age when they can fend for themselves. This is a long process. It takes 40 to 45 days for Golden Eagle eggs to hatch, and a further 80 days must elapse before the young can leave the nest.

During this time the adult eagles are easily disturbed and although they will attack any creature that approaches too close, a persistent intruder will cause them to abandon the nest entirely. Small birds sometimes harass eagles into leaving their eggs or helpless young.

Hunting strategy

The eagle hunts by quartering its territory, flying in an apparently leisurely fashion back and forth until it identifies a target. The attack begins as a dive in which the bird gains flying speed. It pulls out of its dive to approach the target at a shallow angle and very high speed. At the last moment the legs are swung forward to seize the prey, which is snatched and carried away to a place where it can be eaten in safety.

The final stage of the attack is so swift that the victim is unlikely to see its attacker at all. If it does, escape is not difficult since the bird is committed to its run and cannot change direction, so if it misses it will have to overshoot, climb, and commence an entirely new attack, by which time the alerted prey may have found cover. A Golden Eagle will take any animal up to the size of a small lamb and although eagles have been persecuted as sheep-stealers, it is probable that they take only the slow-moving, sickly lambs that might die anyway.

Winged wolves

The rare Harpy Eagles, or Harpies are among the most fearsome of hunters. They can be distinguished by a ruff of feathers on the head and are sometimes called 'winged wolves'. The true Harpy (*Harpia harpyja*) lives in the tropical forests of South America, where it has had to modify the typical hunting techniques of all eagles because there is insufficient space among the trees to permit free flight. It spends much of its time above the tree canopy, seeking birds and monkeys in the topmost branches, but

Top:
A Harpy Eagle with its chick on the large nest it has built high in the tropical forests of South America.

Above:
This Wedge-tail Eagle (*Aquila audax*) has caught a rabbit which it is holding in its powerful talons.

Apart from the American vultures, such as the condor, which belong to the family Cathartidae, and the Secretary Bird, there are three families of birds of prey: the eagles, hawks and Old World vultures (Accipitridae), the falcons (Falconidae) and, in a family of its own, the Osprey (Pandionidae).

Eagles

The eagles live in remote places, among mountains. Typical eagles, such as the

at lower levels it will sit motionless on a branch, watching for movement, then launch itself into a short range attack. It is not as fast as a Golden Eagle, but it will take tree-dwelling mammals up to the size of a sloth.

The sea eagles and serpent eagles have no feathers on the lower part of their legs. They feed mainly on fish or reptiles, but these may be caught from inland waters as well as from the sea. The American Bald Eagle (*Haliaetus leucocephalus*) is a typical sea eagle and derives its name from the white plumage on its head and neck – it is not bald. The African Fish Eagle (*H. vocifer*) resembles the Bald Eagle, but its white plumage extends over its breast and the upper part of its back.

The Osprey, or Fish Hawk (*Pandion haliaetus*) resembles the eagles in some ways, but is dark above and white below, has long, narrow, angled wings and hunts for fish by hovering, then plunging vertically, feet first.

The falcons also hover. There are more than 35 species in the genus *Falco*, and the Falconidae family has about 60 members. The Peregrine (*Falco peregrinus*), known in America as the Duck Hawk, was the bird most popular among falconers because it is easy to tame and can be taught to retrieve its prey. It was always the female that was preferred for falconry.

The Peregrine can be up to 48 centimetres (19 inches) long. The smaller Kestrel (*F. tinnunculus*) is common all over Europe and is often to be seen perched on trees or telegraph poles or hovering over the verges beside main roads.

All the Falconiformes hunt by day. At night their place is taken by the Strigiformes, the owls, birds that are superficially similar to the Falconiformes, but are not related to them closely.

Top:
The Osprey eats only fish and so always nests close to water, making a large nest of sticks in a high tree, cliff or ruined building or, occasionally, on the ground.

Above:
The Peregrine Falcon is the bird most often used in falconry. It is easy to tame and with careful training it will learn to kill selected prey. The hood covers its eyes to calm it and prevent it from being distracted by the sight of small birds and animals it is not required to hunt.

71

Below:
The Elf Owl of North America sometimes nests in hollow trees, emerging at night to hunt animals.

Bottom:
The Eagle Owl flies silently on its nightly hunting forays for roosting birds and small mammals.

Opposite, top:
The Barn Owl also hunts silently by night and can catch its quarry in complete darkness.

Opposite bottom:
A bird's bill and feet help it in its particular way of life. The wood-pecker has strong claws for gripping a tree firmly and its bill is a strong, sharp chisel for chipping away at bark. The gannet has webbed feet for swimming and a bill it can use to seize fish. The eagle has strong talons for gripping prey and the sharp, curved upper mandible of its bill is used to tear meat.

Hunters of the night

Owls are well adapted for nocturnal hunting. They have very large eyes, directed forward. The efficiency of an eye depends on the number of rods and cones on the retina, which resolve detail, and on the size of the cornea, which admits light. The eye of an owl is as large as it can be and it occupies a large part of the skull. It can be moved in its socket only to a limited extent because of its size, so that an owl must turn its head to follow a movement. Its hearing is acute, the external opening to the ear being large and complex in construction. In some species the ear openings are arranged at different levels, which may give them stereophonic hearing. They fly silently, their wing feathers being covered with down that muffles the sound of flapping. They hunt for small nocturnal animals of all kinds which they seize in their talons, like eagles, using their bills to tear food to pieces if the prey is too large to be swallowed whole. Everything is swallowed: bones, fur, feathers and all, the indigestible parts being vomited out later as pellets.

There are two families of owls, those that have no visible ear tufts (Tytonidae) such as the Barn Owl (*Tyto alba*), and those with ear tufts (Strigidae) like the Eagle Owl (*Bubo bubo*). There are 11 species of Tytonidae and 123 species of Strigidae, distributed all over the world.

Owls vary greatly in size. The North American Elf Owl (*Micrathene whitneyi*) is less than 13 centimetres (5 inches) long, not much bigger than a sparrow, while the Eagle Owl is much larger than a buzzard, measuring 70 centimetres (27$\frac{1}{2}$ inches) or more from bill to tail. The Eagle Owl will kill an animal the size of a young fawn.

Owls are birds of the night, but in very

high latitudes this lifestyle causes difficulties. In summer, when food is most plentiful, the nights are very short and an animal that hunted only during the hours of darkness would find it difficult to survive. The Snowy Owl (*Nyctea scandiaca*) has resolved the problem by changing its behaviour and hunting by day. Although the Snowy Owl lives in the Arctic, it occurs widely in Canada and every few years the species migrates south into the northern parts of Europe. Their size, colour and behaviour, especially their habit of chasing smaller birds, may cause them to be mistaken for Gyrfalcons (*Falco rusticolus*). However the owl has a larger head and rounder wings than the falcon and like all owls it appears to have no neck. It is usually alone and often perches on rocks or posts from which it can maintain its watch, for its favourite prey, the lemming.

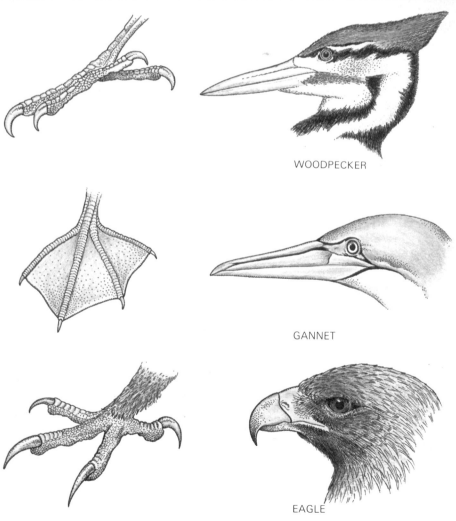

WOODPECKER

GANNET

EAGLE

Carnivorous mammals

Invertebrate eaters

In the rivers of eastern Australia and Tasmania, crayfish, snails and other invertebrate animals are hunted by the most primitive of all mammals, the Platypus (*Ornithorhynchus anatinus*), an animal up to 50 centimetres (nearly 20 inches) long with a bill like a duck and a tail like a beaver. It suckles its young, although it has no teats, the milk being secreted into its short fur, from which the young lick and suck it. The Platypus retains some reptilian characteristics: it lays eggs, like those of certain lizards, and on its hind legs the male has spurs concealing fangs connected to a poison gland. Its venom is mild and probably this inoffensive animal uses it only in fights between males at mating time, but its possession is more typical of a reptile than of a mammal.

The Platypus is a Monotreme as are the Spiny Anteaters (family Tachyglossidae). These animals look like hedgehogs and, unlike the semi-aquatic Platypus, they are wholly terrestrial. They lay eggs and suckle their young, though, and have poison fangs concealed in spurs on the hind legs. They feed on ants which they dig for with their strong claws and seek out with their long, sensitive snouts.

The long snout is typical of anteaters. The Numbat, or Banded Anteater (*Myrmecobius fasciatus*) has one. It is an Australian marsupial. Marsupials occur in Australasia and nearby islands and in the

Americas, where they include the common oppossums. The young are born alive but spend several months inside a pouch in their mother's body.

The true anteaters are placental mammals, whose heads are extended into long, tubular muzzles, with weak jaws and tiny mouths. They are toothless and have long, worm-like tongues, coated with sticky saliva, that they use to collect their prey. Anteaters of the New World belong to the order Edentata and those of the Old World to the orders Pholidota and Tubu-

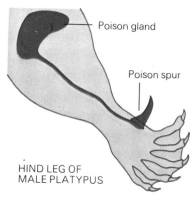

Poison gland

Poison spur

HIND LEG OF MALE PLATYPUS

Opposite:
The Grizzly is the most feared of all bears and one of the largest. One blow from a forepaw can kill a cow and a bear is strong enough to carry the cow back to its den. Much of the grizzly's diet is vegetarian, but it will eat meat readily.

Above:
The Platypus feeds on crayfish, snails and other invertebrates that it finds on the bottom of rivers in Australia and Tasmania.

Left:
The Numbat is about the size of a rat and feeds on termites and ants. Its snout is long and pointed.

Right:
Opossums are the only marsupials that still survive in the New World. They live mainly in trees and feed on small mammals and reptiles, invertebrates, eggs and nestlings, and a variety of plant foods.

Below:
The Aardvark burrows very rapidly and its strong claws can break open the hardest of baked earth to seek out termites and ants which it captures on its 45 centimetre (18 inch) long tongue.

Bottom:
Armadillos are great burrowers, being able to vanish into the ground to avoid danger. They feed on a mixed diet of insects, worms, small vertebrates, carrion and roots and fruit.

Opposite top:
The Sun Bear is the smallest of all bears and because it feeds mainly on insects it has no real need for large, strong teeth.

Opposite bottom:
The American Brown Bear eats a variety of animals, including fish, which it catches by standing in the water and flicking fish on to the bank with a forepaw.

lidentata. The New World species include the Giant Anteater (*Myrmecophaga tridactyla*) of South America, an animal measuring about 1.2 metres (4 foot) from nose to the base of its tail, which adds another 60 centimetres (2 foot) or so. It has powerful claws on its front feet, used for climbing, for tearing into ant and termite nests, and for fighting. The claws are so large that the anteater has to turn them in and walk on the sides of its feet. The Lesser Anteater or Tamandua (*Tamandua tetradactyla*) is about half the size of the Giant Anteater and lives mainly in trees.

The anteaters are related to many extinct species and to the modern sloths and armadillos. The armadillos (family Dasypodidae) are more omnivorous, but they, too, have sticky tongues to help them catch ants, termites and other small creatures. There are 20 species of armadillos, of which the most common is the Peba, or Ninebanded Armadillo (*Dasypus novemcinctus*). Armadillos are protected by horny plates at the shoulders and hips joined by bands of plates that move against one another; the Peba has nine such bands. Armadillos roll themselves up to evade injury, but they are also powerful diggers. The Peba is not the best, but it can vanish into hard ground in less than two minutes, burying itself as a means of escape from danger. It is often considered as helpful to the farmer, for despite its digging, it lives on insects and their larvae, worms and millipedes.

In the Old World, the pangolins (order Pholidota) resemble the New World armadillos but instead of plates they have overlapping scales that do not cover the face or underside of the body. Pangolins live on ants, some being tree-dwellers, others living on the ground.

The largest of the insectivorous mammals is the African Aardvark, or Earth Pig (*Orycteropus afer*). About 1.2 metres (4 feet) long with a 60 centimetres (2 foot) tail, it digs burrows to find ants. It is the only member of the order Tubulidentata.

The familiar Hedgehog (*Erinaceus europaeus*) is also an insect-eater, a member of the order Insectivora, together with the shrews and moles. Savi's Pygmy Shrew (*Suncus etruscus*) is not only the smallest member of the order, it is the smallest of all mammals, measuring no more than about 40 millimetres ($1\frac{1}{2}$ inches) from nose to the tip of its tail. The largest insectivore is the Moon Rat (*Echinosorex gymnurus*), an Asiatic hairy hedgehog up to 45 centimetres ($17\frac{1}{2}$ inches) long, not counting the tail, that lives on insects, fish and reptiles.

Carnivores

It is not only the small and primitive mammals that dine on insects – so do some bears. The Honey, or Sloth Bear (*Melursus ursinus*) lives in forest and grassland areas of India, Assam and Ceylon. It is a nocturnal animal about 1.5 metres (5 feet) long which likes to augment its mainly vegetarian diet by digging a hole in an ant or termite nest and sucking up the occupants. The Sun Bear (*Helarctos malayanus*), also called the Malay Bear or Bruang, breaks open the nest with its paw and allows the insects to climb over the paw, then licks them up. It is the smallest of all bears, growing to only about one metre (39 inches) long, and like many bears it suffers badly from tooth decay, caused by the many sweet things it enjoys eating.

Bears are not insectivores, but carnivores, members of the same order (Carnivora) as the cats, dogs and weasels. Most bears are omnivorous and although they are rather shy and seldom attack humans, all of them are dangerous if provoked. The largest of the bears, and the most feared because of its uncertain temper, is the Grizzly Bear (*Ursus horribilis*), which can be more than 2.75 metres (9 feet) long and can weigh nearly 700 kilograms (1,543 pounds).

The Grizzly Bear lives in North America and like its relative the Black Bear (*U. americanus*) it will dig for small burrowing animals. Bears are methodical creatures and will dig up a hillside so thoroughly that it looks like a ploughed field. Bear tracks are paths made by bears as they move about their range and a bear will always use an existing track if it can, never stepping to either side if it can help it.

Arctic hunters

The one species that is wholly carnivorous is the Polar Bear (*Thalarctos maritimus*), an animal about the same size as the Grizzly that has adapted to life in the Arctic. Its fur extends to cover its feet, which are very broad to spread its weight when walking on ice and to help it keep its footing on slippery surfaces. Its large size is part of its adaptation to a cold climate, its total body surface area being less than that of a smaller animal in proportion to its volume, so that heat loss is reduced. Its small external ears also help reduce heat loss. Like all bears it is a strong swimmer, using only its front legs for propulsion and trailing its hind legs and using them as a rudder.

In summer, Polar Bears can be found far to the south of the permanent ice, feeding on berries and other plant material, but their staple food is the meat of the seal. A Polar Bear cannot outswim a seal, but sometimes it will hunt one in the water, driving the seal into a corner from which escape is impossible. More usually, though, the seal is hunted on the surface. If a hungry bear sees a seal it will stalk it with great patience, taking advantage of any cover – some people say that a stalking bear will even

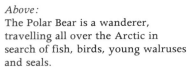
Above:
The Polar Bear is a wanderer, travelling all over the Arctic in search of fish, birds, young walruses and seals.

Above right:
African Hunting Dogs are savage predators. As a pack they can bring down a wildebeest but a single individual is still a formidable hunter.

Below:
Jackals hunt mainly by night and because they work in packs they are able to take prey much larger than themselves. They will also eat carrion and follow lions to take the remains of their meal.

place snow on its black snout to improve its camouflage. Within striking distance, the bear is fast and surprisingly agile and a blow from its front paw will break the neck of a seal. At other times, the Polar Bear will wait for its prey to surface to breathe at one of the holes seals make in the ice. To make sure it is waiting by the right hole, the bear will find the other holes and close them with ice and snow. When the seal appears, it is killed with a single blow, then seized and dragged up through the breathing hole with so much force that its pelvis may be crushed.

Polar Bears are solitary, like most bears, and although they do not hibernate in the true sense, they accumulate a thick layer of body fat during the summer on which they subsist during the winter, when they spend much of their time sleeping.

Wild dogs

The dog was the first animal to be domesticated by Man, in an arrangement that probably began when groups of men and groups of dogs found themselves hunting together. The dogs helped the men, in return for which they received protection and a share of the catch. When times were hard, no doubt the men ate the dogs.

The ancestor of the modern domestic dog was probably a small Asiatic wolf and all present-day dogs, like wolves, are members of the genus *Canus*. All domestic dogs belong to one species, *Canus familiaris*. The jackals of southern Europe, Africa and Asia are close relatives, the Common Jackal (*C. aureus*) being a grey-yellow animal about 60 centimetres (2 feet) long with a bushy tail. The Australian Dingo (*C. dingo*) was introduced by settlers from what is now Malaysia, and it ran wild. The American Coyote (*C. latrans*) is a native animal that has managed to hold its own against competition from the more powerful wolf.

The African Hunting Dog (*Lyctaon pictus*) is a more distant relative, as are the Dhole (*Cuon javanicus*) of Asia and the Bush Dog (*Speothos venaticus*) of Central and South America.

Group co-operation

Many dogs, including the wolves from which domestic dogs are descended, are social animals, living and hunting in packs, usually consisting of about six males and females plus their young. Each breeding season the previous year's litter leaves the pack to form new packs. The pack has a central den, surrounded by a territory, sometimes of as much as 3,000 square kilometres (1,158 square miles). The males mark out the territory by urinating on trees or rocks that the animals pass regularly. Among themselves, members of a pack live peacefully, with an established social order, but strangers are likely to be attacked and when two strange animals meet they approach one another with great caution.

When hunting, members of the pack separate. When an animal finds prey it brings it down if it can and then howls to summon the others to share the food, the leader always eating first. If the quarry is too large to be dealt with by one animal, it howls to summon help.

Co-operation of this kind is essential if an

animal the size of a wolf is to hunt on the open grasslands, where much of the game consists of large grazing animals, and where competition for the smaller animals is keen. If wolves were to feed on ground squirrels, say, or other small animals, they would need to catch very large numbers to satisfy their hunger. This might be possible were it not for the fact that the enemies of small mammals include snakes and weasels that can pursue them into their burrows, and birds that can swoop on them with much greater speed than any dog can manage. So far as the herbivores are concerned, large size is an advantage in that it reduces the number of predators. A wolf is the only animal that will attack a caribou, for example, but it can do so only by working as a team with other members of the pack.

Above:
Once a tame dog introduced by early settlers, the Dingo today is completely wild and hunts in packs. This pair have killed a wallaby.

Below:
Wolves are the largest of the wild dogs. In winter, when they are more dependent for food on large animals, wolf packs are at their largest. In summer the packs usually disband.

The wolf pack

When a wolf pack finds a particularly rich source of food it may carry co-operation so far as to summon other neighbouring packs to share the kill and the feast. In this way the pack can recruit additional hunters that may be necessary when dealing with a large herd. Eskimos say they can tell from the howls and yaps of the wolves when packs are being summoned to a migrating caribou herd, and this is a signal for the men to begin their own hunt.

Unlike many mammals, dogs have no breeding season. Cubs may be born at any time of the year and since not all the members of a pack will be reproducing at the same time, the care of the cubs is the responsibility of the pack as a whole. This reduces the number of adults that are needed to supervise and protect the young, and allows more to take part in the hunt.

The African hunting dog has a somewhat similar social organisation, but unlike the wolf it is nomadic and hunts mainly at dawn or dusk, to avoid the heat of the African day. Its packs are larger than those of wolves, numbering 12 to 20 adult animals. The hunting dogs live on the savannah grasslands and hunt gazelles and animals as large as zebra and wildebeest.

To hunt in the open, both stealth and speed are required. Hunting dogs will move slowly towards a herd of their prey, trying to approach to less than 50 metres (164 feet) without causing a stampede. After that they run, different dogs abandoning the main chase for animals that are too fast for them and turning to slower animals, so that the hunt may end with many dogs pursuing one victim.

Dogs kill by biting, and all dogs have very powerful jaws, teeth designed for piercing and shearing, and a wide gape. They will attack the throat if they can, to ensure a quick kill, but if the prey is too large for them to reach the throat they will attack the soft underparts.

The behaviour of the prey is curious. They know when hunters are hunting by their general attitude and posture. Dogs adopt a slightly crouching posture, for example, with the head held low. This causes alarm, but when they are not hunting, wolves can wander among a herd of caribou and be ignored. The herd will remain alarmed until one of their number has been killed, when they will resume grazing very quickly.

The coyote, no less maligned by humans, is more solitary than the wolf. It is a nocturnal animal, spending much of the day in a burrow which it digs or takes over from badgers or prairie dogs. It mates for life and family groups sometimes collaborate in hunting, running in relays, when they can maintain speeds of 60 kilometres (37 miles) per hour. Like the

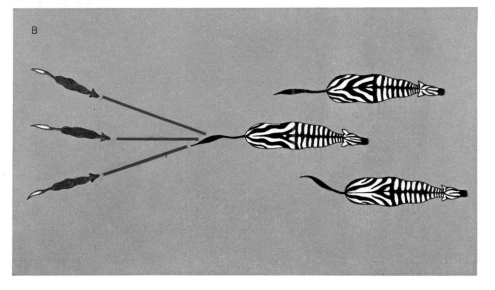

jackals, the coyote lives on a varied diet of small animals and carrion, and it also eats some fruit and vegetables, especially juniper berries, rose hips and cactus.

Foxes will also eat fruit and vegetables as well as carrion and they have learned to survive in cities, subsisting mainly on what they can find in dustbins. They are skilled and efficient hunters, though, and by killing rodents and rabbits, their principal prey, they help control populations of species that humans regard as vermin.

The fox is a nocturnal animal, hunting mainly at dawn and dusk, when it will stalk its prey with great patience. It has keen senses of hearing, sight and smell. It lives a solitary life, pairs remaining together only until the cubs have been taught to hunt for themselves, during which time the family lives in a den made from a burrow dug by another species and enlarged to suit the foxes.

Foxes will kill domestic poultry and they like eating eggs. They have acquired a bad reputation because of their habit of 'overkill', when they kill far more poultry than they can eat. Probably, this behaviour is caused by the panic among the confined birds that stimulates the killing instinct of the fox. Were the birds able to escape it is unlikely that the fox would attempt to pursue them once it had secured its meal.

The hyenas (family Hyaenidae) look like dogs, but in fact they are related more closely to the cats and belong to the superfamily Feloidea. The Striped Hyena (*Hyaena hyaena*) of parts of Asia and Africa is about the same size as a wolf. The Brown Hyena (*H. brunnea*) of southern Africa is larger. Hyenas have very long forelegs and powerful jaws that can crush large bones. Despite their reputation, they are anything but cowardly and although they eat carrion they will also hunt big game, sometimes competing for it with lions. They are solitary animals and although a number may share a carcase, they do not collaborate in hunting as do dogs.

The Aardwolf (*Protelas cristatus*) is the only member of a subfamily (Protelinae) of the hyena family. It is smaller than a hyena and has weak jaws with widely spaced, identical, peg-like teeth that are different from those of any other carnivore. It lives on carrion, ants and termites that it collects on its sticky tongue.

Above:
Hyenas are more closely related to cats than to dogs and although they are often seen in groups they do not collaborate in hunting. These Spotted, or Laughing Hyenas (*Crocuta crocuta*) of Africa, south of the Sahara, live in clans of up to 100 animals, dominated by females and feeding mainly by scavenging during the daytime and hunting at night.

The cat family

The cat superfamily includes the civets and cats as well as the hyenas. The cats (Felidae) fall into two main groups. If a cat purrs it belongs to the genus *Felis*, if it roars it belongs to the *Panthera*. The Cheetah (*Acinonux jubatus*) purrs, but it differs from other cats in other ways, the most obvious being that its claws cannot be retracted.

The small cats (*Felis*) include the Domestic Cat and its wild ancestors the African Wild Cat (*F. lybica*) as well as animals as large as the Puma (*F. concolor*). The big cats (*Panthera*) include the Tiger (*P. tigris*) and Lion (*P. leo*).

The lynxes (*Lynx*) form a smaller group within the small cats, and include the Northern Lynxes (*L. lynx* and *L. canadensis*). These are forest animals that will kill an animal the size of a small deer. *L. lynx* is the largest wild cat of Europe. The Bobcat (*L. rufus*) is smaller than the lynx. It lives in the North American forests and deserts.

Unchallenged killers

Cats, except the Lion, hunt and live alone. The Lion lives on the grasslands and hunts animals larger than itself. The Cheetah, which hunts in similar terrain, can run fast enough to catch its prey in a short chase,

Above:
The Leopard hunts on the ground but once it has killed its prey it carries it into a tree where it can eat in peace and where leftovers can be stored for future attention.

Above right:
The Cheetah is a cat with feet like those of a dog. It cannot retract its claws. Its hard footpads and long legs help it run fast and its claws give it the grip needed for sudden turns and stops, so that in its final attack the Cheetah is able to catch and bring down small antelopes and other fast-moving animals.

Right:
The North American Bobcat resembles a domestic cat but is very much larger. It feeds on small animals of all kinds, but it is not certain that this one will catch its Snowshoe Rabbit, which has made a run for it. A cat may catch a rabbit by stalking and pouncing, but it stands little chance of running one down.

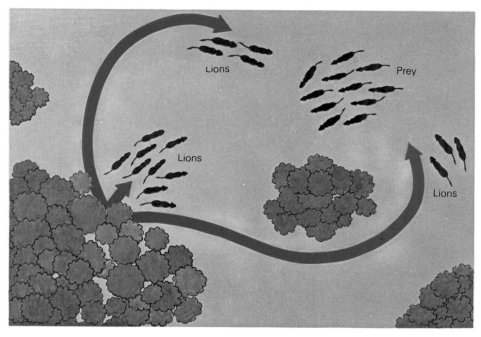

but the Lion is not a fast runner. So, like the dogs, it relies on teamwork, although this is not so highly developed as among the hunting dogs.

A pride of Lions usually consists of several females with their cubs, often a cubless female, and one or two males. Sometimes lions hunt by day, but usually the day is spent resting and grooming. At dusk the roars of the males arouse the pride to the night's hunting and they roar again at dawn to signal the beginning of the day.

The hunting is done by the females and they usually work alone, stalking their prey by sight and hearing until they are close enough to charge. They rely on stealth and a very swift, close-range attack, and must be able to bring down their prey quickly, before it can escape.

Lionesses have often been seen hunting in groups. One group will hide in the scrub downwind of a herd of prey, while a second group moves upwind and behaves aggressively, to stampede the prey into the ambush.

Lions breed at any time of year and by living in groups it is possible for the cubs to be fed and protected from predators such as hyenas.

Above:
Lions sometimes co-operate in hunting. One group hiding down wind of the prey while the others drive the prey into the ambush.

Below:
Lions are the only cats that collaborate in hunting and they live in groups of from three to 30. These lions are eating an animal that may have been killed by a single blow from a forepaw, which can break the neck of an animal the size of a zebra. In the background is Mount Kilimanjaro.

Smaller carnivores

The weasels, stoats and ferrets (family
Mustelidae) are among the smaller carnivores, but they may be the most determined of hunters. The Stoat (*Mustela
erminea*), Weasel (*M. nivalis*) and Domesticated Ferret (*M. eversmanni furo*) are barely
larger than the rodents they catch, and
much smaller than the rabbits that form an
important part of their diet. The many
species of badgers are members of the same
family, the European Badger (*Meles meles*)
eating grain and plants as well as animals of
all kinds. The largest of the weasel family,
however, is the Wolverine (*Gulo gulo*), an
animal rather more than one metre (39
inches) long that lives in the Arctic tundra,
where it has a hunting territory that may
cover more than 250 square kilometres (62

square miles) for each individual. A Wolverine will kill an injured elk and in a fight with a lynx or bear it is quite likely to win. Its name means 'glutton' and is derived from its habit of storing surplus food.

Marsupial carnivores

Over most of the world the placental mammals have proved more successful than more primitive mammals and have supplanted them. Australia, however, became isolated from other land masses after the arrival of marsupials but before the arrival of placentals, probably more than 80 million years ago. Although marsupials survive in the Americas it is only in Australia and some adjacent islands that they have filled all the roles played elsewhere by placental species. Thus there are marsupial carnivores (family Dasyuridae) including 'cats'.

The 'cats' range in size from the little Northern Cat (*Dasyurus hallucatus*), about 28 centimetres (11 inches) excluding the tail, which feeds on insects, small mammals and birds, to the Tiger Cat (*D. viverrinus*) which is about 60 centimetres (24 inches) long and feeds on mammals and birds.

The Tasmanian Devil (*Sarcophilus harrisii*), a nocturnal animal with strong jaws and teeth, and a wide mouth gape, has been persecuted by Man, but its numbers are recovering. It feeds on carrion, but its chief victims are sheep.

Man the hunter

Walk along the bank of any river or canal where the water is reasonably clean and you are almost certain to see people fishing with rod and line. Walk through the countryside at certain times of year and you will hear the sound of gunfire. Farmers shoot pests to control their populations, but many people shoot wild or semi-wild birds for enjoyment. In countries with a rich wildlife, hunters are licensed to shoot larger game, under a system of strict rationing.

Man has always hunted. We are omnivorous and although we can live perfectly

Below:
The Tasmanian Devil is about the size of a fox. It feeds on small mammals and birds as well as invertebrates and carrion and it has been accused of killing domestic animals. It is solitary and hunts mainly by night.

Left:
Despite its larger size and its venom, the Indian Cobra stands little chance against the Indian Mongoose (*Herpestes edwardsii*). If the snake bites the mongoose the mongoose will probably die, but as the snake strikes, the mongoose darts out of reach and immediately springs back to seize the snake by the head and crush its skull. Mongooses hunt many small animals besides snakes.

Above:
In the hands of a skilled hunter the blowpipe can deliver a dart with great accuracy over a short range, it is usually tipped with a poison.

Below:
Coastal eskimos are very dependent on the sea. This man is attaching a rope to the walrus he has killed so he can tow it home.

well without meat, we enjoy eating it and always have.

For early Man this presented problems. A man cannot run fast enough to catch his prey, even in a short dash. If he manages to seize a large animal he has no claws to hold it. His mouth does not open wide enough, his jaws are not strong enough, and his teeth are not sharp enough to kill it. If it should fight back he can do little to defend himself. So man could never hunt in the way most predators hunt. He could obtain some meat by scavenging, and sometimes a party of humans might rush a rival carnivore and steal its food, but this was always dangerous and uncertain.

Man's tools were his hands, eyes and brain. His hands were adapted for gripping and his forward-looking eyes gave him binocular vision, characteristics inherited from his tree-dwelling ancestors and shared with other primates. His large brain enabled him to devise implements for his hands to hold, weapons that would serve as claws and teeth and that would provide him with greater speed. He threw stones and sticks, and the throwing stick acquired a sharp point and became the spear. He invented the bow and blowpipe to deliver missiles and he learned to dip these in poisons that would incapacitate his quarry. He learned to stalk skilfully and, from the start, his hunting parties worked as teams. Even so, hunting was an inefficient way of providing meat and while many hunting peoples took only about one-third of the meat available to them, so allowing an adequate breeding population to survive and replenish the stock, in some places the very inefficiency of hunting caused great damage. Entire herds of cattle were driven over cliffs to supply the very few carcases

the tribe could use before the meat became putrid.

The introduction of modern firearms improved the efficiency of hunting, often with disastrous consequences. Game was killed in huge numbers. William Cody, perhaps better known as 'Buffalo Bill', once shot 250 bison in a single day, and he claimed to have killed 4,280 in 17 months. Some Eskimo tribes starved when they killed so many of the animals on which they depended that game almost disappeared.

Hunting industries

The only modern industries based on hunting are whaling, seal-hunting and commercial fisheries, and in each of these, the introduction of modern technologies threatens the survival of the stocks.

This is only one response to the inefficiency of hunting. The other, which began about 12,000 years ago, was to domesticate the most useful meat animals. Today almost all the meat we eat is provided by livestock farmers from herds and flocks far more numerous than those of their wild ancestors. Man the hunter became Man the farmer.

Apart from whalers, seal-hunters and fishermen, the modern huntsman hunts for sport, often using a primitive method. Yet despite his natural disadvantages and lack of armament, Man has long been the most voracious predator on earth.

Above:
The North American Bison almost became extinct through over-hunting in the 19th century, because men on horseback equipped with firearms were able to kill far more than the Plains Indians, who hunted on foot with bows and arrows.

Below left:
The Sperm Whale may become extinct through hunting.

Below:
Today a ship powered by large diesel engines uses electronics to locate a shoal and a trawl net can hold many tons of fish.

Right:
Although its movements on land are clumsy, the Clawless Otter is a marvellous diver and swimmer. It usually hunts from the bank, spotting its prey and diving upon it with great accuracy.

Above:
The Sea Otter uses a flat stone as a tool, floating on its back with the stone on its chest and breaking shellfish, such as this sea urchin, on it.

The return to the sea

In some of the rivers of tropical Africa there live small animals that look very like otters. The largest of them is about 35 centimetres (13¾ inches) long. Look at one closely, however, and you will see that it does not have webbed feet. This is only one feature that distinguishes it from the true otters and in fact it is not even a close relative. It is the Otter Shrew (*Potamogale velox*), a member of the insectivore order and related to the shrews and moles. It hunts for small fish and other aquatic animals, and it is one of the mammals that has returned, at least partly, to the water from which all life emerged.

The true otters belong to the weasel family. The Common or River Otter of Europe and Asia (*Lutra lutra*) is typical. It is found by lakes and streams, is very active and intelligent, and hunts fish and small animals of all kinds. It swims strongly and can stay submerged long enough to swim 400 metres (1,312 feet) or so. Sometimes it ventures into the sea.

The marine otters are rather different and more completely adapted to life in the sea. The hind legs have been modified to form flippers and the Sea Otter (*Enhydra lutris*) comes ashore very rarely. The young are born at sea and sea otters are said to sleep tangled in seaweed that prevents them from drifting away from their companions. They live in herds of up to 100 animals. They have fewer teeth than River Otters and feed mainly on shellfish for which they dive 30 metres (98 feet) or more to the sea bed. They are one of the few species to use tools, breaking open clam shells with flat stones that they hold while floating on their backs. Like all the otter subfamily (Lutrinae) they are very playful. There are two species, both found in the Pacific, the Sea Otter and the smaller Marine Otter (*Lutra felina*), the sea otter being confined to the northern hemisphere, the marine otter to the southern.

The marine otters are in some ways more completely aquatic than the seals, which must come ashore to mate, to give birth to

Left:
Fur seals sunning themselves on a
sandy beach at Cape Cross, Namibia.

their young, to moult, and sometimes just to rest. Yet in other ways the seals have adapted to marine life more fully. Their limbs have become flippers. The front flippers conceal fingers that are joined together but leaving separate claws. The hind flippers have webbed toes. The body is streamlined and insulated against heat loss. Seals usually remain in coastal waters, although they have been encountered as much as 50 kilometres (31 miles) from the shore.

Seals and sea lions

Seals, sea lions and walruses form the order Pinnepedia, or 'fin feet'. These carnivorous mammals returned to life in the sea long ago, presumably because conditions on land were less favourable to them. There are three families and the first of them to have returned to the sea, about 50 million years ago, were probably the true seals (Phocidae), distinguished by their lack of external ears and their thick layer of blubber. They live in temperate and cold waters and at some time during their expansion they must have crossed the Equator, because they occur in both hemispheres. Their hind flippers point backward and have become a kind of tail and they swim moving these flippers from side to side, first one flipper then the other.

There are 18 species of them, the Common or Harbour Seal (*Phoca vitulina*) being one of the most common. The largest of the true seals are the elephant seals of northern and southern seas. The bulls are very much larger than the cows, but a Southern Elephant Seal (*Mirounga leonina*) bull can reach a length of 6 metres (19½ feet). This immense bulk and the modification of the hind limbs to make a substitute for a tail makes elephant seals very cumbersome on land and they climb out of the water only with difficulty.

The eared seals (family Otariidae) on the other hand, have external ears and swim using their forelimbs. The hind limbs can be swung forward on land, which makes them much more mobile than the true

seals. The family consists of the sea lions, whose most famous representative is the Californian Sea Lion (*Zalophus californianus*), and the fur seals. Most are found in warm waters, although the Kerguelen Fur Seal (*Arctocephalus tropicalis*) is an Antarctic species and the Northern Fur Seal (*Callorhinus ursinus*) is found as far north as the Bering Sea.

The walruses (family Odobenidae) live in the Arctic. They have tusks, which are fearsome weapons, and live on fish, crustaceans and molluscs. Their large, strong teeth are able to crack the toughest shell.

It is possible that the pinnipeds are changing evolutionarily, and the larger of them may be close to the point at which they will be unable to leave the sea at all because they are too cumbersome. If this is so, they may be following the path made many years earlier by the cetaceans, which are the most completely aquatic of all mammals.

Above:
Walruses can swing their hind limbs forward on land, but they also use them in swimming. The tusks are used as weapons, but walruses also use them to help pull themselves along on land and to support their head on rocks – or occasionally on boats, with disastrous consequences – while they are resting. The walrus is the only animal that walks on its teeth!

The whales

The order Cetacea includes all the whales, animals that returned to the sea about 65 million years ago and that have solved all the problems attendant on life in the sea. Indeed, people once thought they were fishes.

There are 92 species of cetaceans, found all over the world, including what is believed to be the largest animal ever to live on Earth and the only mammal capable of diving to the deep sea bed. The Blue Whale (*Balaenoptera musculus*) can reach more than 30 metres (98½ feet) in length, and the

Above:
Sperm Whales diving, off the coast of California.

Right:
Sea lions and sheathbills watch as an Orca, or Killer Whale, swims close to the shore.

Sperm Whale (*Physeter catodon*) is known to dive to more than 1,100 metres (3,609 feet). All cetaceans are highly intelligent, playful and sociable, and some species have highly developed means of communication.

The whales can be divided into two suborders, those with teeth (Odontoceti) and those without (Mysticeti).

The dolphins (subfamily Delphininae) are toothed whales usually 1.5 to 3 metres (5 to 10 feet) long. There are 30 species of true dolphins and they are found in all seas. Dolphins are a fairly common sight. They live in schools or family groups and many seem fascinated by human activities. The species you are most likely to see in northern coastal waters is the Common Porpoise (*Phocaena phocaena*), about 1.8 metres (6 feet) long and one of the smallest of whales. The Common Dolphin (*Delphinus delphis*) and Bottle-nosed Dolphin (*Tursiops truncatus*) are also numerous. They feed on fish, crustaceans and squid and have few enemies apart from sharks and their relative, the Orca.

The Orca (*Orcinus orca*), traditionally called the Killer Whale or Grampus, grows up to 9 metres (29½ feet) long and is a fearless hunter of aquatic animals of all kinds, including some of the larger whales. Orcas live and hunt in groups but despite their aggressive reputation they seem well disposed toward Man. They hunt only for food and are very intelligent, far removed from the mindless killers of legend.

The largest of the toothed whales is the Sperm Whale, which can grow to nearly

20 metres (65½ feet). It dives to great depths and can remain submerged for more than an hour. It feeds mainly on large squid and apart from human whalers its only enemy appears to be the giant squid. It is possible that there are squids large enough to kill a Sperm Whale. Sperm Whales live in groups of up to 20, usually moving slowly close to the surface, although they can swim at more than 30 kilometres (18½ miles) per hour when being pursued.

The Narwhal (*Monodon monoceros*) is a toothed whale which lives in the Arctic and northern coastal waters. The males have curious tusks formed from the upper right canine tooth that grows forward in an anti-clockwise spiral to a length of up to 2 metres (6½ feet). No one knows the purpose of this tusk. The narwhal feeds on cephalopods and molluscs.

Giants of the ocean

The giants of the oceans are the baleen, or toothless whales, animals that feed on the small animals that form part of the plankton, floating close to the surface, and especially on a small crustacean, very high in protein, called krill. A Blue Whale eats about four tons of krill a day.

Baleen whales have huge mouths with a very wide gape. When the mouth is open, large triangular plates of horny material, called baleen, hang down to form a screen against which food is trapped as the whale draws water into its mouth. The water is expelled when the whale moves its tongue, and the food is swallowed. A Blue Whale may have as many as 700 baleen plates.

Above:
These Bottle-nosed Dolphins, 'porpoising' in the Pacific off the Galápagos Islands, feed on fish, crustaceans and squid. They are very intelligent. Some people believe they may be as intelligent as Man.

Can the hunters survive?

Above:
The Polar Bear, like most large predators, has few enemies other than Man. It has been hunted for centuries for food, for its fur, and simply as a hunting trophy. Today it is protected from hunting but may suffer the loss of part of its habitat as the Arctic is opened up for development.

Below:
This Sea Otter lives off the California coast. After becoming almost extinct through hunting for their fur, the Northern Sea Otters are now safe from extinction, but the numbers of those off California are recovering only slowly.

In the past 200 years, 200 species of mammals and birds have become extinct, most of them because of Man's activities. Man has hunted them for their meat, skins or other products, persecuted them because he believed them to be pests, and starved them by taking from them the land on which they lived. The pressure on wildlife is increasing. The world's leading conservation body, the International Union for Conservation of Nature and Natural Resources announced in 1977 that there were 257 species of mammals, 348 species of birds, 186 species of reptiles, and 30,000 species of plants that face extinction in the near future.

In the early 1960s, Tigers were fairly common in India. Today there may be no more than 5,000 in the whole world. Crocodilians are farmed on a small scale in the USA, but the outlook for wild specimens is very uncertain. Their skins make handbags and shoes that are just too attractive. Of the marine mammals described in the previous chapter, the species in danger of extinction include five otters including both marine otters, 11 baleen whales, three fur seals, one sea lion, the Atlantic walrus, and six true seals. The Polar Bear, which is almost a marine mammal, is also rare.

The effect of hunting is obvious, but difficult to halt. Whaling, for example, is an industry using very expensive equipment that must be paid for, and the protection of the species it exploits usually seems less important than the income that pays the wages.

While the demand for furs and skins remains high, a tribal hunter can earn what is to him a large income from poaching. Of course, predators are hunted no more than other animals, but they are especially vulnerable, because the hunting of herbivores reduces their food supply, so that long before the hunted herbivores face extinction, the predators have gone. The clearing of land for human use may reduce hunting territories. Again, enough herbivores may survive to continue the species, but there may be too few to support the predators that depend on them. Without the predator the prey may survive, but without its prey the predator is doomed.

Many animals will abandon nests or breeding grounds if they are disturbed. In regions popular for tourists the habitat may be preserved, but the constant presence of humans, even well-meaning ones, drives away all but the hardiest species.

Effects of pollution

Some predators, especially the birds of prey, have suffered badly from pollution. Substances such as those used as pesticides remain for a time in the body of any animal that swallows them. An insect may acquire a dose of pesticide from the plant that it eats. A bird that eats insects acquires some of this poison from each insect it eats. A bird of prey then eats the small birds and acquires some pesticide from each of its victims, and this accumulated poison may be large enough to harm it.

In most cases extinction is not inevitable. The use of such dangerous pesticides was reduced greatly and the birds of prey recovered. We can change the way we do things and allow other species to share the planet with Man. It is up to us.

Captive predators

In the 12th century BC, the Chinese Emperor Wen opened a garden near his palace in which he kept specimens of wild animals from all over his empire. His may have been the first zoological garden. Since then, zoos have been kept in almost every great city.

The justification for zoos, especially for those occupying valuable land in cities, has always been partly entertainment. They have been criticised for this. People wonder whether it is right to capture wild animals, for no better reason than to provide Sunday afternoon amusement for people with no real interest in wildlife. On the other hand, much of our knowledge of the anatomy of wild animals has been derived from zoo specimens.

More recently zoos have begun to fill a much more important role and one that is likely to increase in years to come. A modern zoo, well equipped and managed and staffed by workers who understand and care about the animals in their charge, can provide the only remaining refuge for species that face extinction. Of course it is

Below left:
Most countries have laws to protect wild animals from poaching, but the enforcement of these laws is often difficult, when a tribesman can earn what to him is a fabulous sum simply by killing and skinning an animal. These jaguar skins have been seized by the authorities in the Amazonas region of Brazil, but so long as the rich demand furs, poaching is likely to continue.

Below
The Tiger is now protected, and reserves are being established in various parts of India, Bangladesh and Bhutan where it can live in peace.

Top:
As humans learn to respect and protect other species, so animals lose their fear of men. These lions are feeding on an animal they have killed, unconcerned by the tourists who have stopped to watch them.

Above:
In modern zoos and game parks the animals have right of way and can roam free. For this baboon the notice is simply a convenient place to sit and watch the world go by.

Below:
The marine mammals are popular entertainers, allowing people to marvel at their strength and skill. But do such displays enhance respect for the animals?

Below right:
The creation of national parks and reserves allows game to be observed and studied. These wildebeest are migrating across the Serengeti Plains in Tanzania.

better for species to survive naturally, in the wild, but survival in captivity is better than no survival at all. Extinction is permanent. Several species have been rescued in this way. Père David's Deer (*Elaphurus davidianus*), for example, is found in many zoos, but *only* in zoos. It has been extinct in the wild for more than a century.

Sometimes species that have been rescued can be re-introduced to the wild, but this is much more difficult than it may seem. Many species are threatened because humans have taken over their territory. Unless their territory is restored to them their re-introduction is futile. If we tried to bring the wolf back to Britain, how would it survive? Certainly it would consume large numbers of rabbits and other small animals, but wolves must live in packs and they could not hope to kill enough rabbits to feed themselves. Hunger would force them

to kill sheep and cattle and their extermination as pests would begin all over again. Bears would face the same problem. The lynx, on the other hand, hunts only small mammals and birds, and is shy and frightened of humans. Perhaps it could be re-introduced. Of the larger predators, Lions have been re-introduced to the wild successfully as have Tigers.

It is never simple and many things can go wrong. When a species leaves a particular area its place is soon taken by another. If man does not replace it, either directly by taking the food it used to eat or indirectly by clearing away the original wild community and substituting his own crops, then some other species will. In nature, food is not left uneaten for long. A predator re-introduced to a changed habitat may fail to compete or it may survive only by making new changes, as wolves would do in somewhere like Devon, England.

If the habitat can support the species, then introduction may succeed, provided the animal can support itself. Animals reared, and possibly bred, in captivity may lose the hunting skills and detailed knowledge of their environment that are essential to their survival. They may have to face, accept and be accepted by others of their own species. So re-introductions always proceed slowly and carefully. The animals must be fed and possibly protected until they have learned to fend for themselves. Yet it is well worth the effort. Every animal re-introduced successfully means that the possible extinction of one species has at least been postponed.

Index

Textual reference is in Roman and captions to illustrations in Bold.